W9-AHO-834

VANISHING
POINT

The Disappearance of Judge Crater,
and the New York He Left Behind

□

RICHARD J. TOFEL

Ivan R. Dee   Chicago   2004

Library of Congress Cataloging-in-Publication Data:
Tofel, Richard J., 1957–
  Vanishing point : the disappearance of Judge Crater and the New York he left behind / Richard J. Tofel.
    p. cm.
  Includes bibliographical references and index.
  ISBN 1-56663-605-1 (alk. paper)
  1. Crater, Joseph Force, b. 1889. 2. Judges—New York (State)—New York—Biography. 3. Missing persons—New York (State)—New York—Case studies. 4. New York (N.Y.)—Politics and government—1898–1951.
I. Title.
  KF373.C68T64 2004
  347.747'014'092—dc22

                                              2004052669

For my father,
and in memory of my mother

CONTENTS

New York is too rich to be brought to insolvency. Great cities, when badly administered, cannot be sold and abolished; they simply become dirty, unhealthy, unsafe, disgraceful, and expensive.

—E. L. GODKIN

There is no denying that the government of cities is the one conspicuous failure of the United States.

—JAMES BRYCE

PREFACE

☐ There is an enduring mystery at the heart of this tale, but this is not altogether a "mystery story." It is also an account of how the disappearance in 1930 of one man, New York State Supreme Court Justice Joseph Force Crater, became emblematic of the decline and fall of Tammany Hall, the New York County Democratic party machine. Crater was a stalwart of that machine, and this is the story of how Crater and Tammany approached the vanishing point together.

Judge Crater's fate became perhaps the most celebrated missing persons case of the last century. It has never been resolved. The New York City Police Department spent nearly 50 years, off and on, trying to find Crater before they gave up. By then, Judge Crater would have been 90 years old; today he would be 115.

The search for Crater absorbed the attention of New Yorkers in a way nearly impossible to comprehend. And this even though Crater had not been well known outside legal and political circles before he vanished, and it had been less than six months since Governor Franklin Roosevelt, in a surprise move, had named Crater to the bench. Yet, in just the first month after Crater was reported missing, the *New York Times* devoted fourteen front-page articles to the hunt for the judge and the implications of his disappearance. Moreover, the *Times*, as usual, was more restrained than its competitors.

But Judge Crater has never been the subject of a book—that is, if we don't count a slim volume by Mrs. Crater, written more than forty years ago. As we shall see, she was not the most reliable witness, nor the least self-interested.

What follows, then, is not a definitive solution to the Crater mystery, although it is possible to make educated guesses about what may have happened to him—and to note what almost certainly did not. Nor is there a single "suspect" identified here, although it can be established that some people, including individuals ostensibly close to Crater—some of them very important, then and later—do not seem to have been terribly eager to have him found.

Exploring the disappearance of Crater involves a close look at political life in the city of New York in the years when the Jazz Age gave way to the Great Depression. Across this stage strode men such as:

- former Governor Al Smith, still licking his wounds from a presidential campaign seemingly decided by religious bigotry, and striving to maintain his influence over Tammany and with the people;
- Governor Roosevelt, the man who had first called Smith "the Happy Warrior," now off and running for

president himself, and coping with a problematic relationship with the party machine that already went back twenty years;

- Smith's former legislative colleague, U.S. Senator Robert F. Wagner, founder of a New York dynasty that the Crater story might have threatened in its infancy;
- Mayor James J. Walker, "Gentleman Jimmy," for whom Crater's disappearance would be the beginning of the end; and
- Fiorello H. La Guardia, trounced by Walker in the most recent mayoral election but still restless and ambitious, the man who would eventually seize this moment to set New York on a new path.

They are all here; they all played their parts.

When they and others were done, Joseph Force Crater was almost certainly dead. Beyond that, Tammany Hall was vanquished, and New York was embarked on the longest period of reform government in its modern history.

We begin with Joseph Crater at his end, and, in particular, with the first week of August 1930. But then, before exploring the Crater mystery in greater depth, it is important to set the wider scene of Tammany's world, and the challenges that Tammany faced as Joe Crater reached the vanishing point. The two stories then come together—as a result of which both, finally, come apart.

Vanishing Point

Chapter One

THE WORLD
HE LEFT BEHIND

☐ It was a summer Friday, August 1, 1930. United States Senator Robert F. Wagner was at work at his firm's New York City law office at 120 Broadway, near City Hall. Wagner, formerly the State Senate majority leader, had been elected to the U.S. Senate in 1926, but that was not a full-time job. Congress was out of session more often than not.

Wagner had established the law firm in 1927, just after his election, and was joined in it by Simon Rifkind (who also served him as a Senate aide) and Francis J. Quillinan, the son-in-law of New York's then-governor, Alfred E. Smith. By 1930 the firm was known as Wagner, Quillinan & Rifkind.

Wagner, a German immigrant most of whose family had long since returned to the old country, was due to sail on the

North German Lloyd line the next day to begin his annual European vacation. This afternoon he received a visit from New York State Supreme Court Justice Joseph Force Crater. The judge came to wish the senator *bon voyage*.

The setting was familiar to Crater—until just a few months earlier he too had practiced law out of the Wagner firm's offices, leasing space for his own work and serving as the firm's counsel in many appellate cases. And the two men's association was one of long standing. Ten years earlier, in June 1920, Crater, then just thirty-one years old, had gone to work as law secretary for Wagner, then himself a justice of the state Supreme Court.

New York's Supreme Court is not the state's highest tribunal but its main trial-level court. Law secretaries, now just as then, are Supreme Court justices' key employees—in many other courts they would be called clerks. But while clerks are often very young, just out of school, law secretaries in the New York State trial courts are often more experienced. They serve administrative and other staff functions as well as providing research assistance. And while most judicial clerks serve only one- or two-year terms, law secretaries often remain with their judges for much longer periods, establishing much deeper associations. Crater began working for Wagner when he was already four years out of Columbia Law School, and stayed in the job for six years.

In 1926, shortly after Justice Wagner ascended from the trial court to the Supreme Court's Appellate Division, the middle-level court in the New York system, Joe Crater was replaced as Wagner's law secretary by Rifkind, a twenty-five-year-old Lithuanian immigrant and Columbia Law graduate whom Crater had selected for the post.

Much later, Wagner said of his encounter that afternoon with Crater, "Our chat was quite good-humored and informal." Crater said goodbye to Wagner, who was expected to be in Europe for a month. The judge then climbed into his own chauffeur-driven Cadillac and headed for his lakeside vacation cabin near Belgrade Lakes, Maine. It was Crater's second or third visit of the summer to Belgrade Lakes, a town north of Lewiston, near the center of the state, and the seasonal home that he and his wife, Stella Mance Wheeler Crater, had owned for eleven years and had been visiting since 1916. Crater was returning to Maine after two weeks in New York and Atlantic City.

Early on the morning of Saturday, August 2, after driving through the night, Crater and his chauffeur, Fred Kahler, stopped for breakfast at a hotel in Augusta, Maine. Soon they reached Belgrade Lakes, where Crater joined his wife. The couple had no children.

The Craters spent Saturday going motor-boating with local friends, eating dinner out, and bowling that evening in the village. At some point during the day the judge took the time to write and post a $90 check to a woman he knew back in New York. By all accounts, Crater seemed carefree; he told his neighbor Ludwig Traube that he intended to stay in Maine for two or three weeks. But that night, apparently after making or receiving a telephone call in town (their home didn't have a phone), Crater told his wife that he had to leave to attend to a pressing matter in New York. He would depart the next day, he said, but promised to return on Wednesday, the 6th, and in any event no later than the following Saturday, August 9—Stella's forty-third birthday.

On Sunday, August 3, Fred Kahler drove the judge to the train. (Crater did not know how to drive.) Crater had promised to take a trunk to the railway express for his niece, Harriet Clarke, who was off to summer camp. He did, but he forgot to prepay the shipping charges. The next morning, back in New York, he went to the City Hall post office annex and mailed his niece money to pay the freight.

Back in town, Crater went to his apartment in a fashionable building at 40 Fifth Avenue. He had purchased the co-operative apartment for $13,500 in 1927 ($140,000 in today's money); the maintenance, for upkeep and utilities, in 1930 was $136 per month, or about $1,500 today. Once there, Crater spoke to the housemaid, a woman named Amedia Christian, and asked that she return to tidy up after his departure, on Thursday the 7th. After that, he told her, they wouldn't be needing her for a few weeks, until Monday the 25th; that was the day he was due back in New York again for the opening of the Supreme Court term.

After freshening up at home, Crater went to work in his chambers at the courthouse in Foley Square, near City Hall. He lunched Monday at a nearby restaurant, located at Broadway and Chambers Street, and visited his physician, Dr. Albert Raggi. Crater had badly injured his right index finger when a car door was slammed on it during his late-July visit to Atlantic City; two weeks later the finger was still described as "somewhat mutilated, due to having been recently crushed."

That evening, Crater, an avid theatergoer, went to see *Ladies All*, which billed itself as "a spicy comedy." He was joined by his friend William Klein, the attorney for the Shubert theater organization. After the show Crater, joined by Klein or perhaps by attorney Frederick Kaplan, or both men, moved on to the Club Abbey on West Fifty-fourth Street.

There the judge spent some moments with Elaine Dawn, a singer and dancer who had recently appeared in *Show Boat* and *Artists and Models*.

Stella Crater later described Club Abbey as "a night club of sordid reputation which, Joe told me, he visited for 'political reasons.'" The *New York World* described the Abbey as a "white light rendezvous" and "one of the smart club places in the fifties."

Club Abbey was owned by Owen "Owney" Madden. Madden, a Liverpool native, had been a gang leader in his youth, later a leading bootlegger, an occasional backer of Broadway shows (including Mae West's *Sex*), and a fellow with a violent past. Indeed, he was widely known in the underworld as "Owney the Killer." In 1912, Madden had shot and killed a man; it was almost certainly not his first homicide. Two years later he had ordered the killing of another, and had been convicted of manslaughter and sentenced to twenty years in prison. He was released in less than half that time, and, perhaps sensing the opportunities presented by prohibition, appears to have sworn off killing. Instead he "bankrolled himself . . . by a few judicious armed robberies" and went into business as a club owner and bootlegger. His Club Abbey was frequented by such like-minded criminals as Jack "Legs" Diamond, Dutch Schulz, and Vincent "Mad Dog" Coll. Judge Joseph Crater visited the club at least twice, and likely quite a bit more often than that.

The next day, Tuesday, August 5, Judge Crater lunched with a colleague, Justice Alfred Frankenthaler, and perhaps also with Justice Louis Valente, the chief judge of his court. At some point Tuesday he wrote a check for $50 to the Broadway Temple Methodist Episcopal Church, fulfilling part of a $250 pledge he had made three years earlier when he had encountered the church's pastor in Senator Wagner's office. The church was the same one at which the Craters had been married in 1917, although they had long since stopped attending.

Later the judge went to the home of Dr. Raggi at 130 West Eleventh Street, relatively near his own apartment, for dinner and an evening of poker. It ended between midnight and one o'clock in the morning. According to later accounts, Crater's poker style was conservative: ". . . He did not toss in many chips. He was a shrewd and cautious player, seldom bluffing, and when he raised his friends knew that he had sufficient to win. His complaints, when they withdrew from the pot, were always delivered in a serio-comic tone that was one of his best-known characteristics at the club." When the poker game ended, Crater returned home for what would turn out to be his last night in his own bed.

☐   Wednesday, August 6, 1930, was the fourth consecutive day of ninety-degree temperatures in New York. The low for the day was seventy-five degrees, at 8 A.M. The heat drove 200,000 New Yorkers to the Rockaway beaches. Three local residents died of heat stroke during the day; another four drowned seeking refuge in the waters surrounding the city.

The heat served to remind New Yorkers of a more severe weather problem facing much of the nation's interior—a terrible drought. A milk industry spokesman observed that "Conditions in the agricultural regions are the worst in decades, [with] bleak sun-baked acres of ruined crops and panting helpless cattle." Corn topped a dollar a bushel for the first time in more than a year. But at least one man saw a hidden blessing in this fact. Henry A. Wallace, the Iowa publisher (and future U.S. vice president), suggested for the newspapers of August 6 that "A year or two from now, when we look back, we shall see that the drought was the first definite thing which happened to stop the depression of 1930 and start the process the other way."

It was already clear that the market decline of nine months earlier had foretold a "depression"—of the sort, perhaps, seen in 1921 or 1907. Wednesday was an important day for reporting corporate results, and the news was almost uniformly bad. General Motors said second-quarter operating net income had fallen 41 percent, and first-half results 35 percent, although the company had nonetheless earned $53 million in the quarter and more than $98 million for the six months. Woolworth announced that sales for the month of July had fallen 7.2 percent from a year earlier. And Woolworth was not alone: J. C. Penney saw July sales fall 6.6 percent, though they were still up 2.5 percent for the year to date.

On the New York Stock Exchange it was a slow day. Just 1,317,370 shares changed hands, fewer than one-tenth as many as had traded on Black Thursday ten months earlier. The Dow Jones Industrial Average fell four points this August day, to close at 234.38—down 61 percent from its pre-crash high, but up 18 percent from its post-crash low. In Great Britain it was announced that the ranks of the unemployed now topped 2 million, more than twice the level of a year earlier. In the U.S., 3 million people had been out of work as the year began; the number now stood closer to 5 million.

Economic activity was not nearly at a standstill, however—not yet. The Empire State Building, the monument of former governor Al Smith, was rising at his urging. By August 6 it was 55 stories tall, and more than 3,400 men were employed in the effort to build it. The *Daily News*, the pictorial tabloid that had taken the New York newspaper market by storm since its introduction in 1919, had just recently moved into a monument of its own, an Art Deco tower on Forty-second Street.

The pressing question in partisan politics was not what to do about the economy but whether to repeal prohibition, now in its twelfth year. Everywhere, it seemed, the battle lines were drawn between "wets" and "drys," with the wets seemingly ascendant. Their cause was being championed in New York State Republican ranks by no less than Columbia University president Nicholas Murray Butler. And the issue was well on its way to being settled in New York: votes had gone 4 to 1 for local option repeal as early as 1926; in New York City the vote was 7 to 1. In Virginia, a forty-seven-year-old local judge named Howard Smith, unacceptable to dry forces in the Old Dominion, nevertheless won a contested Democratic primary for Congress—tantamount to election. Thursday would bring a primary in Tennessee, in which it was expected that Congressman (and former Democratic National Committee chairman) Cordell Hull would move on toward the U.S. Senate.

"Judge" Howard Smith would spend the next thirty-seven years on Capitol Hill supporting a rearguard action in defense of the racial status quo, but elsewhere on August 6 there were signs that this status quo was eroding. Dr. Simon Drew, the "Negro Billy Sunday," was honored in Harlem on his sixtieth birthday and took the occasion to praise New

York governor Franklin D. Roosevelt. Blacks, Dr. Drew said, appreciated the attention Governor Roosevelt had paid them, and might be enticed by him away from their traditional home in the party of Lincoln. "Such a man" as Roosevelt, the preacher noted, "would be fitting for President of the United States." Indeed, Roosevelt was already the front-runner for the 1932 Democratic presidential nomination.

For his part, FDR spent the day relaxing on the yacht of his friend Van Lear Black, as it lay at anchor in Long Island Sound. Nine years earlier Black, now publisher of the *Baltimore Sun*, had employed Roosevelt briefly as a banker. Roosevelt might have had mixed feelings sailing with Black—he had done so off the coast of Maine in 1921, just a day before first showing the symptoms of his polio.

"Negro" leaders other than Dr. Drew weren't waiting for the 1932 elections to seek progress in race relations. Oscar De Priest, a congressman from Chicago and the first black to serve in Congress in twenty-seven years, continued his apparently futile efforts to place young men of his race in the service academies at West Point and Annapolis. The third black De Priest named to the military academy, Benton J. Brooks, Jr., failed the physical because of a "bad heart" and left the Point that Wednesday.

The opposition faced by men such as Brooks and De Priest was considerable. Help-wanted advertisements on the front page of the *New York Herald Tribune* specified the desired race of the future employee: a white "housemaker . . . German type preferred" in New Rochelle, a "colored" cook in Suffern.

In the wider world, however, this sort of narrow-minded cynicism gave way to nearly unbridled idealism, much of it remnant of the Great War, in this, the eleventh year of the peace. The same front page of the *Herald Tribune* carried a daily thought from the nation's immediate past president, "Calvin Coolidge Says." Coolidge termed French Foreign Minister Aristide Briand's call for a "confederation of Europe" "probably premature" but "interestingly suggestive." And Congressman Fiorello La Guardia was this day returning from London, where he had done his own bit for utopianism at the Interparliamentary Conference. Only the stubborn insurrection of the Chinese Communists seemed to mar global politics.

It was not enough to distract most New Yorkers. Silk stockings were on sale at Lord & Taylor and Wanamaker's for a dollar a pair. Men's suits at Rogers Peet were $30, or $35 at Saks. Macy's offered a portable phonograph for just $9.94. Median family spending in the city was running at $3,000 for the year.

For those seeking spectator diversions, the Brooklyn Dodgers, known universally as the "Robins" after Wilbert Robinson, their manager since 1914, offered some promise. Having not won a pennant since 1920, the Robins beat Pittsburgh that August 6 and remained in first place by three and a half games. (Real Brooklyn fans knew better; the team eventually finished fourth.)

The Robins' crosstown National League rivals did something even more unusual that night—they played ball. Night baseball had first come to the minor leagues earlier in the 1930 season. On Wednesday, August 6, John McGraw's Giants played their first night exhibition game, against the Bridgeport Eastern League team before eight thousand fans in Bridgeport. (Bill Terry, leading all major league hitters at .407, was there, but McGraw stayed behind in New York.)

In the American League, the Washington Senators beat the Philadelphia Athletics, but the A's retained their six-and-a-half-game lead and were on their way to their second World Series championship in a row. The Yankees, even with Lou Gehrig batting .381 and Bill Dickey .362, were no match for a Connie Mack squad led by Al Simmons, Jimmie Foxx, Mickey Cochrane, and Lefty Grove.

Sports fans who thought it was too hot to enjoy baseball might have found some respite in the news that Eleanor Holm had chosen this day to set a new world's record in the 150-yard women's backstroke.

In addition to *Dancing Partner*, a new comedy produced by David Belasco, theatergoers were lining up to see Douglas Fairbanks, Jr., in the film *Dawn Patrol*, while other fans of the talkies could see Frank Capra's *Rain or Shine*, Victor Fleming's *Common Clay*, or Howard Hughes's *Hell's Angels*, which opened Tuesday night. The Hughes film was being touted as "the first multi-million dollar talking picture."

Those more daring looked skyward for their diversions. Frank Hawks, piloting a Curtiss pursuit plane, spent the day setting an east-to-west transcontinental air record of fourteen hours, fifty minutes, forty-three seconds, making five stops en route from New York to Los Angeles. It was expected that Hawks, on his return flight, would eclipse Col. Charles Lindbergh's west-to-east record.

For his part, Lindbergh seemed content to let Hawks have the records. "Lucky Lindy" spent part of the day aloft with his wife. Ninety minutes in their Lockheed Sirius monoplane marked their first flight together since the birth of their son, Charles A., III—the "Lindbergh baby"— in June.

Mrs. Lindbergh was a budding poet as well as an aviator, but today's literary news concerned others. From Montgomery, Alabama, came word that the local Kiwanis Club had elected H. L. Mencken a member. Mencken was scheduled to marry a Montgomery girl, Miss Sara Powell Haardt, on September 3. Meanwhile, in New York, Donald Freide, the publisher of Theodore Dreiser's *American Tragedy*, announced that he would appeal a $300 obscenity fine levied against the book.

On a less profane note, President and Mrs. Herbert Hoover must have spent the day saddened by the death of Msgr. Ramon Mestres, the pastor of the Carmel, California Mission, and the man who had officiated at their 1899 wedding. The choice had been made by the future Mrs. Hoover, a Monterey native, who had sought and received dispensation to have the Catholic priest unite the Methodist bride and Quaker groom. New York City in 1930 was no less polyglot: 37 percent Protestant, 34 percent Catholic, 27 percent Jewish, with 2 percent of the population Eastern Orthodox. While the black population of the city had quintupled in the thirty years since the turn of the twentieth century, it stood at less than 350,000 out of a total of nearly 7 million.

☐   All these events provided the background to a gathering upheaval in the judiciary and politics of the City of New York.

On August 6, testimony at the municipal corruption trial of "Horse Doctor" William Doyle showed that deposits in Doyle's bank accounts had exceeded his reported income for three years in a row. And the differences were hardly minor:

	reported income	deposits
1927	$59,740	$278,787
1928	42,286	158,974
1929	57,915	179,582

Doyle had come a long way from his days as a Fire Department veterinarian. When the department was motorized, Doyle used political connections to gain a transfer to the Bureau of Fire Prevention. He retired from that post after being indicted for failing to enforce the fire code in a building that later burned. But the curtain soon rose on this third act—as a practitioner before the city's Board of Standards and Appeals, seeking waivers of various regulations. On at least forty-nine separate occasions, he managed to persuade the board to overturn prior rulings. As a contemporary journalist put it, "He was, of course, a broker in political chicanery; he admitted under oath later that he had split his rich fees [with officials of the agencies before which he practiced], but no investigating agency was ever able to force him to divulge the identity of his partners in bribery. Since he took most of his fees in cash the money could not be traced."

On the same day Doyle's deposits were being compared to his salary, Mayor James J. Walker suspended Tammany Hall district leader Martin Healy as first deputy commissioner of Plants and Structures. It must have been a painful moment for the mayor; he and Healy had been boyhood friends and had served together in the State Assembly as young men in 1918–1919. But Healy had left Walker little choice. Thomas Tommaney, the chief clerk to the sheriff of

New York County, had just become the third person to invoke his privilege against self-incrimination in a grand jury investigation of whether Healy had sold a judgeship to Magistrate George Ewald.

Despite the three witnesses' refuge in the Fifth Amendment, testimony by others had already established the outlines of the transaction. In March 1927, George Ewald's second wife, Bertha, had cashed a check from her father in the amount of $5,000. She had also withdrawn money from her childrens' trust funds. On April 26, Mrs. Ewald had written Tommaney a certified check for $5,000. The next day, as Ewald's court appointment was announced, Healy made a $5,000 cash deposit to his own account. One week later, Healy made another $5,000 deposit, this one by certified check. Total payments: $10,000, a bit more than the $8,500 increase in Ewald's salary from his previous post as a deputy assistant district attorney.

But the Ewald–Healy grand jury was not done. Among the witnesses slated to testify on August 7 was Tammany district leader John Mara, father of Joseph Mara, one of Joseph Crater's closest associates. And Joseph Crater was president of Tammany's Cayuga Club, the club in which Martin Healy was district leader.*

☐ Judge Crater returned to his chambers at about ten o'clock on Wednesday morning, August 6. What he was working on is not known, but it is likely that politics rather than law absorbed

---

*Clubs were the focus of Tammany's organization at the assembly-district level, the level closest to the voters. Each district had one or more leaders who served as Tammany captains.

his attention. Only one, relatively trivial, case was pending on his docket, but he was expected to run for a full fourteen-year term as a Supreme Court justice in the fall.

Some time that morning, Crater asked Joseph Mara, his confidential assistant, to cash two checks and bring the cash back to him. One was for $3,000 drawn on his account at the Chase National Bank, the other for $2,150 drawn on an another account, at the Empire Trust Company. The Empire Trust check left $12,000 remaining in Crater's account there, but the Chase account was nearly cleared out. (Later Mara lied about the amount of the Chase check, but eventually he admitted that he had cashed both checks for the amounts stated.) Crater received a brief visit from Simon Rifkind, perhaps while Mara was out cashing the checks. There is no record of what they discussed.

When Mara returned, Crater asked for his help in lugging to the Crater apartment six portfolios of assorted papers. The cases Mara and Crater used for the purpose were later found in the apartment, but the papers themselves were not. Crater also spent some time that morning destroying other papers.

Leaving chambers, Crater told his law secretary, Fred Johnson, that he was planning to go up to Westchester for a swim, presumably as a means of relief from the stifling heat of the day. (Between 11 A.M. and 1 P.M., the temperature in midtown had risen from eighty to eighty-seven degrees.) Dismissing Mara after the papers had been delivered to his apartment, the judge again mentioned going up to Westchester for a swim. Mara and Johnson both assumed Crater meant that he was planning to visit the Larchmont Shore Club, of which he was a member. While not a strong swimmer, Crater was fond of the water. The club, however, later indicated that Crater did not appear, and indeed had not visited its premises since June.

Instead Crater, as was his custom once or twice a week, had lunch at the Epicure Restaurant on Stone Street with attorney Martin Lippman. Later, at around 5:30 P.M., the judge telephoned an attorney, Reginald Issacs, about a case. Issacs owed Crater $1,000 in connection with a legal matter from Crater's days in practice, but it is not known if they talked about this. At some point in the afternoon Crater had changed his clothes, putting aside the suit he had worn in the morning to be sent to the cleaners, and putting on a brown suit with thin green stripes and the wide lapels he favored. Self-conscious about his unusually thin, size 10 neck, Crater wore a high, stiff collar of the sort still favored by President Hoover but otherwise already moving well out of style. One writer has since noted that Crater "always looked something like a turtle walking upright."

At about 7 P.M., Crater asked at the Arrow Ticket Agency, 1539 Broadway, for a ticket to *Dancing Partner*, the Belasco production of a comedy by Alexander Engel and Alfred Grunwald. The show had opened the previous evening at Belasco's own theater on West Forty-fourth Street, and the *World* had called it "one of those glib brittle, machine-made romances." Crater must have enjoyed it; he had already seen a preview during his Atlantic City visit a few weeks earlier, on which he was accompanied by the Arrow Agency broker Joseph Grainsky. The judge was well known at Arrow, and a clerk later recalled that he said he would be returning to Maine the next day. While at Arrow, Crater also bumped into Frank Bowers, Collector of Revenue and a fellow native of

Easton, Pennsylvania, and the two talked briefly. The agency clerk told Crater that a ticket would be waiting for him at the box office, and a ticket for seat D-110 was left in his name. It was later picked up, but it is not known by whom.

At about eight o'clock that evening, Crater entered Billy Haas's restaurant at 332 West Forty-fifth Street. There, already having dinner, were Shubert lawyer William Klein and the showgirl Sally Lou Ritz (*nee* Ritzi). They invited the judge to join them, and he did so. Crater ate lobster cocktail as an appetizer, chicken and vegetables for his main course, and pie for dessert, all washed down with coffee. Showtime for *Dancing Partner* was 8:40 P.M., but the dinner did not conclude until about 9:15. Perhaps Crater, having already seen the show once, was unconcerned.

The standard account of this tale says that Crater then hailed a cab down Forty-fifth Street, headed toward Ninth Avenue. That is curious on at least two scores: first, it would have left him driving in the opposite direction from the theater to which he was ostensibly headed; and second, it would have placed him in a very warm and uncomfortable automobile, with the temperature still at eighty-six degrees, when he could easily have walked just a few blocks to his destination. Moreover, extensive inquiry later failed to turn up any cab driver who had picked up the judge.

That is almost certainly because there was no such cab. The image of Crater hailing a taxi comes from Klein's initial testimony in a later grand jury inquiry—testimony that made little mention of Sally Lou Ritz. But her account of the situation differed. She and Klein, she reported, left the curb outside the restaurant first, getting into a cab and heading off together to Coney Island. She saw Judge Crater standing there as they left. Faced with this, Klein changed his story, to say that Crater had moved off toward Broadway, and seemed to be hailing a cab. But it is not clear how Klein could have seen such a thing as he headed away from Broadway down the side street—and the illogic of Crater seeking a taxi remains.

Yet, if we can be confident that Crater did not hail a cab, we cannot be at all sure of what he did do. Did he go to the theater? We don't know. Did he return to Club Abbey? Elaine Dawn recalls two evenings there with him, and other witnesses said they saw him there twice with Klein, but one of these nights could have been the previous week, before his trip to Maine, and Klein was off to Coney Island with Miss Ritz.

The fact is that Joseph Crater's trail runs cold at Billy Haas's restaurant. After his dinner there, no one has convincingly admitted to having seen him ever again.

Chapter Two

THE WORLD OF
TAMMANY HALL

☐   Tammany Hall, the political machine that made it possible for Joseph Crater to become a judge, began as an organization devoted to preserving the young American republic and extending democracy. Its motto was "Freedom Our Rock"; its causes included expansion of the right to suffrage and an end to the practice of imprisonment for debt. But within three generations, what had begun in idealism became a fount of cynicism.

The Society of Saint Tammany, early on known as the Columbian Order of New York City, was founded in 1786 and incorporated in 1789. In opposition to the elitist Society of the Cincinnati, it opposed hereditary distinctions. The name Tammany was drawn from the Delaware Indian chief Tamanend, who, legend had it, told his tribe to "Stand together. Support each other and you will be a mountain that nobody can move." Despite the subsequent decline and fall of the Delaware nation, that seemed the right sort of fraternal spirit for a political organization in the new United States.

In the face of the Cincinnati's Roman pretensions, the nomenclature of Tammany Hall was *faux* Native American: members rose in ranks from hunter to warrior to sachem. The top officers of the society were the Grand Sachem, assisted by the Sagamore (master of ceremonies) and the Wiskinskie (doorkeeper or sergeant-at-arms). The headquarters of the club was called the Wigwam.

But the purposes of the organization became increasingly partisan, and political in the lowest rather than the highest sense. Within nine years of its incorporation, Tammany was led by the followers of Aaron Burr, whom Alexander Hamilton, before their famous duel, described as "sanguine enough to hope everything; daring enough to attempt everything; wicked enough to scruple nothing." Tammany had begun its march toward being synonymous with the fledgling Democratic party in New York City. The president of the United States was given the honorary title of Great Grand Sachem, or Kitchi Okemaw; this tradition continued through Andrew Jackson, the founding leader of the modern national Democratic party.

Tammany did not abandon its lower-case "d" democratic ideals all at once, but corruption within its ranks, and as a way of life within the society, were increasingly evident even in the Jacksonian era. As early as the 1820s, Grand Sachem Matthew Davis, Burr's chief lieutenant, was convicted of a massive fraud involving banks and insurance companies.

Tammany proved adaptable, however, and thus continued to flourish. Once the province of the privileged, the society soon embraced the immigrants who began to flood New York in the 1840s, and made a tacit (and sometimes explicit) deal with them typical of emerging urban political machines in many locales: financial support, ranging from food to shelter to jobs—indeed, a kind of private welfare system—in exchange for their votes. The Board of Aldermen became widely known as "the Forty Thieves," and by 1854 Tammany had elected as mayor its notorious leader, Fernando Wood. Wood's margin of victory in a close race was supplied by the Sixth Ward, where he received four hundred more votes than there were registered voters. Wood held on to power in part by refusing to enforce a Sunday closing law. A few years later, during the Civil War, he led a group of anti-war Democrats in the city who supported disunion; at one point he actually advocated that the city become a free state. Tammany had now drifted so far from its origins that it had completely abandoned ideology in favor of practicality; public ends took a back seat to private gain.

The man who came to embody Tammany in this era of industrial expansion and social conflict was William Marcy Tweed, its leader from 1860 to 1872. From 1863 on, Tweed was Grand Sachem, but he preferred the simpler title of "Boss," and was the first Tammany leader to be so known. He was also Tammany's last Protestant chief. Tweed took graft to a new level, increasing the expected level of kickbacks on city contracts from 10 to 35 percent, and sometimes as high as 65 percent. From 1840 to 1860, New York's debt had risen 80 percent. From 1860 to 1876, Tammany increased the city's debt sixfold. Tweed and his small group of cronies personally stole an estimated $75 million from New York (roughly $1.1 billion in current dollars) during their dozen-year run. His monument was the so-called Tweed Courthouse. It took ten years to build and cost the city more than $12 million ($175 million today)—forty-nine times the original estimate. It still stands just behind City Hall as a reminder of Tweed's breathtaking ambition.

And his nerve. Tweed was finally driven from power by a coalition of reform elements spearheaded by Samuel Tilden (soon elected governor, and then nearly president, as a result), the editors of the *New York Times*, and the crusading cartoonist Thomas Nast (who adopted the tiger, mascot of Tweed's volunteer fire company, as a voracious symbol for Tammany, just as he created the Republican elephant and the Democratic donkey). Yet when he entered Ludlow Street jail, disgraced and never to emerge, Tweed was asked his occupation and replied, "Statesman!"

But Tammany did not fade with Tweed. It survived and even thrived. As its most noted chronicler, the local leader George Washington Plunkitt, put it in his autobiography, "I seen my opportunities and I took 'em." Some of these, Plunkitt insisted, constituted "honest graft"—ranging from the delivery of actual services by favored contractors at inflated prices, to the creative use of advance notice of government actions, to simple kickbacks. But not all the graft was "honest," even by Plunkitt's standards. Some of the "services," moreover, were better classified as vices. As one early Tammany historian observed,

> New York has always contained a large, pleasure-loving population, whose habits have been somewhat pagan. Any attempts to control too rigidly the desires of this population

were of profit to Tammany men, who were the instruments for safe violation of the law. In return, they received a money consideration. In that way, the moralist was satisfied, for there was the law on the statute books; Tammany men were more than satisfied, for the profits in violating the law were large; and the people who wanted their vices were also satisfied, except that the cost of living that way increased.

And the dishonesty certainly extended to the electoral process itself. One successful local pol, Big Tim Sullivan, described why hirsute voters made the best "repeaters":

"When you've voted 'em with their whiskers on, you take 'em to a barber and scrape off the chin fringe. Then you vote 'em again with side lilacs and a moustache. Then to a barber again, off comes the sides and you vote 'em a third time with the moustache. If that ain't enough and the box can stand a few more ballots, clean off the moustache and vote 'em plain face. That makes every one of 'em good for four votes."

Tammany's march was not entirely unimpeded. The terms of reform mayors William Havemayer, William Strong, Seth Low, and John Purroy Mitchel—the latter three elected on so-called "Fusion" tickets—represented bumps in the road. But they were not more than that. One wag observed that "These reform movements are like queen hornets. They sting you once, and then they die."

Havemayer, recruited again to City Hall more than twenty years after his first term as mayor had ended, died of a stroke in office at the age of eighty. Strong served one term (with Theodore Roosevelt as his police commissioner) but was succeeded by a Tammany acolyte. Low, a former president of Columbia University and mayor of the independent city of Brooklyn, followed but met the same fate, with his term limited to two years. It was Low's re-election defeat that Lincoln Steffens predicted in his classic *The Shame of the Cities*. Mitchel, too, served only one term, and was succeeded by a Tammany man. From the election of Fernando Wood in 1854 through 1930, Tammany had held the mayoralty for all but thirteen of seventy-six years.

In this sway, the nominal opposition, the Republicans, were to some extent complicit. As the Bronx Democratic boss Ed Flynn recalled, the Republicans were so few in number in New York that, "being unable to elect any city official by [themselves, they] lived from 'reform' to 'reform,' [their] bosses keeping themselves alive during the long droughts by accepting handouts from Tammany's back door, [their] nabobs haughtily ignoring the common man between elections."

The most enlightened leader of Tammany was surely Charles Francis Murphy, who ran the machine beginning in 1902 for more than twenty years. Murphy succeeded "Honest John" Kelly (1872–1886), who invented the district leader system so critical to Tammany's electoral successes, and Richard Croker (1886–1901), whose motto was "I am in politics for what I can get out of it."

Like so many Irish political bosses of his era, Murphy was a saloonkeeper. Indeed, the New York of Murphy's coming-of-age seemed a city of saloons. The Bowery boasted eighty-two—six per block. Third Avenue between Fifty-ninth and Ninety-second streets, a thirty-four-block stretch, had eighty saloons. Murphy was also, in the usual Tammany fashion, holder himself of only a minor public post, in his case one four-year term as docks commissioner.

But there the stereotypes ended. Murphy's bars were decorous, and did not admit women. His family life was similarly impeccable; he neither smoked nor drank. In a world of voluble storytellers, he was known as "Silent Charlie," usually confining his responses to political entreaties to "Yes," "No," or "I'll look into it." He left no letters, records, or formal speeches and gave few interviews. He explained that "Most of the troubles of the world could be avoided if men opened their minds instead of their mouths."

He enriched himself, to be sure. By one account, in fact, his wealth increased by $600,000—more than $12.5 million today—just during his four years as docks commissioner. Later he occupied a mansion in town, built a compound on Long Island, "Good Ground," with its own nine-hole golf course, and ended up leaving an estate valued at more than $2 million ($21 million today)—but he managed to do all of this with a certain apparent modesty. The only time he was indicted, for tax evasion, the case was dismissed before trial—by Justice Robert Wagner.

Murphy was the first Tammany leader to dominate politics not only in New York City but in the entire state. But his greatest achievement was that he once again adapted Tammany to the times. A less supple Boss would no doubt have fought the rising urban progressivism of the early twentieth century, would have clung to the formula of food, shelter, and jobs in exchange for votes. But Murphy saw that social welfare legislation could enable Tammany to take the same credit on a mass basis, and win the same loyalty, that it once had to win case by case.

Murphy explained himself once to Frances Perkins, who years later served as FDR's secretary of labor. While executive secretary of the New York Consumer's League, she had persuaded the legislature to pass a bill limiting working hours and was now seeking new building regulations. Referring to the earlier effort, Murphy said,

> "Well, young lady, I was opposed to that bill."
>
> "Yes, so I gathered, Mr. Murphy."
>
> "It is my observation that that bill made us many votes. I will tell the boys to give all the help they can to this new bill."

In all, one contemporary journalist observed, Murphy "forced on his disciplined followers a sense of proportion that was almost as good as a conscience."

Murphy also saw that new methods required new men. He thus advanced the careers of youngsters such as Robert Wagner and Al Smith, whom he made his leaders in Albany at the ages of thirty-three and thirty-seven, respectively. Murphy's deal with them was relatively straightforward: he still controlled patronage jobs and contracts (although Smith, when governor, was later given some leeway on appointments), and Murphy still got to decide which candidates to designate for what office; they could legislate as they pleased. Murphy decreed, "Give the people everything they want." Wagner, in turn, later called Murphy's Tammany Hall "the cradle of modern liberalism in America."

Unfortunately for Tammany, Murphy's sophistication was not shared by his successors, and Murphy's sudden death in 1924, at age sixty-five, proved a watershed. *New York Times* columnist Arthur Krock observed, "The brains went out of Tammany Hall when he died." Smith, now governor, sought to run Tammany from Albany, but could not, as most of the patronage was tied to city rather than state jobs. When Jimmy Walker was elected mayor in 1925, Smith's influence was weakened still further, and by the time Smith lost the presidential election of 1928 his hold on Tammany was virtually nonexistent. Murphy's successor as Grand Sachem, George Olvany, was nearly as weak as Murphy had been strong. Where Murphy had ruled for twenty-two years, Olvany gave up after fewer than five.

The lack of a strong central figure dispersed not only power but any check on that power—or accountability for it. A *New York Times* survey of the state of Tammany in October 1930 found that naming men to minor judicial offices had become a perquisite of district leaders rather than the Grand Sachem. The consequence: "a general belief that such appointments and nominations are bought and sold." And even the position of the district leaders themselves was being diluted. As the population grew faster beyond Manhattan than inside it, the number of assembly districts on the island was cut back. But no leader was willing to surrender his post, and so twenty-three assembly districts now boasted thirty-five district leaders. Meanwhile, all but five of these district leaders also held or had recently held a public job, ranging from member of Congress to deputy commissioner of the Department of Markets.

In the public mind in 1930, the man who most symbolized Tammany Hall was Al Smith. In reality, the machine had moved well beyond him.

☐ Samuel Seabury, who later investigated the corruption surrounding Judge Crater, once said that Al Smith was "the best representative of the worst element in the Democratic Party." What Seabury meant was that Smith was a true reformer—within limits, a proponent of "good government"—but also, always, a loyal Tammany man.

In fact, Smith had begun in politics, in 1894, at age twenty, as an anti-Tammany activist, working for the election of a slate that included Republican William Strong as mayor. Smith's favored candidate for Congress lost, but Strong won, and his new political connections won Smith a fifteen-dollar-a-week job as a process server for the commissioner of jurors. Smith, who later described himself as a "graduate" of the Fulton Fish Market, had grown up on the rough streets of the Lower East Side. His own birthplace was within five blocks of those of both of his parents, his wife, and all of their children. He was younger when he left school than Franklin Roosevelt was when he left the world of private tutors to begin his schooling. Smith recalled his political beginnings this way: "I had a choice of hard labor at a small wage of $10 a week, or $12 at the most, in the kind of jobs that were open to me, or easier work at a greater wage." He never looked back.

When the congressional district squabble in which he had been involved was resolved, Smith remained in politics, making his peace with Tammany. By 1903 he had been marked as a rising star in the neighborhood and was elected to the State Assembly. He was a stranger to Albany—he had never before even seen the state capitol. He recalled, "I was diligent in my attendance at the meetings, but I did not at any time during the session really know what was going on." Named in his second term to the Committee on Banks and the Committee on Public Lands and Forests, he later noted that "I had never been in a bank except to serve a jury notice, and I had never seen a forest."

☐   Smith's roommate in Albany was Robert Wagner, Judge Crater's future mentor. Smith and Wagner rose together in Charles Murphy's machine. In 1911, Smith and Wagner were named as majority leaders of the Assembly and the State Senate, respectively. It was the Democrats' first session in the majority in eighteen years.

Wagner, who sat in the legislature's upper chamber, is nevertheless remembered as the junior partner in this relationship—just as, many years later, he would be Franklin Roosevelt's junior partner in many federal legislative battles. But Wagner had quite a story of his own.

Robert Ferdinand Wagner was born in Nastatten, Germany, the son of a print-and-dye tradesman. The Wagner family came to New York in 1886 when Robert, the youngest of seven children, was nine years old. In order to make his way in the new land, Wagner's father took a job as a janitor; the lure of the post was the basement apartment that came with it. His youngest son, however, excelled almost immediately. He was valedictorian of his high school and then went on to the City College of New York. While he was enrolled there, after ten years in America, his parents gave up and returned to Germany. Robert was put through college—where he also starred as the quarterback of the football team—by his brother Gus, who also remained in New York.

Wagner graduated from City College in 1898 and from the New York Law School in 1900. According to Wagner's biographer, he was quite a young man-about-town: "His taste for good clothes—which developed from the time when, at thirteen, his newsboy profits enabled him to buy his first 'store suit'—lasted throughout his life; photographs [from his mid-twenties] show a handsome young dandy who might have just stepped out of a men's fashion magazine. And Wagner was known to enjoy a drink now and then—quite a few on special occasions."

He took to politics naturally and was elected to the State Assembly in 1904 at the age of twenty-seven. But his loyalty to the Tammany machine, while unwavering, was accompanied by a strong progressive bent. This dichotomy in Wagner's approach to politics may have been reinforced by his defeat, after only one term in the Assembly, by an ostensible "reformer" running under the banner of publisher William Randolph Hearst's Municipal Ownership League. Other explanations for his progressive views are possible, of course, but Wagner "was not an introspective man. Undoubtedly, political expediency counted a good deal for his liberalism. He happened to enter politics just as reform was coming into its own."

In any event, Wagner picked himself up after his defeat and was returned to the Assembly in 1906 when Murphy reached an accommodation with Hearst. Just two years later Wagner moved on to the State Senate, where he became the leader of the majority after only three years.

With the coming of the Great War, however, Wagner was reminded of the different treatment accorded American-born Irishmen like Smith and German-born immigrants like himself. In 1917, with Wagner maneuvering toward Tammany's mayoral nomination, Fusion incumbent John Purroy Mitchel, angry over Wagner's blocking a land exchange in

New York harbor, exploded. "It would appear," the mayor in-
toned, "that certain members of the Legislature are working
in the interest of the German government." Just in case his
listeners were confused, he added, "Of course you know . . .
I mean Bob Wagner."

It was an outrageous charge, and totally spurious, but it
was enough to knock Wagner out of contention for mayor—
and, for a time, to drive him from elective politics altogether.
In 1918, Wagner sought his refuge in election to the state
Supreme Court.

In 1915, Wagner's wife Margaret had been stricken with
a paralyzing illness. In 1919, further weakened by a serious
automobile accident, she died, leaving her husband with a
nine-year-old son, Robert F. Wagner, Jr. In the years to
come, the two Wagner men would live together in a Yorkville
apartment; the senior Wagner never remarried.

Judge Wagner might have been a candidate to succeed
Murphy as leader of Tammany in 1924 and was widely mentioned in that connection. But this time it was Wagner's
Protestant religion, rather than his national origin, that was
deemed to disqualify him. Still, he remained a stalwart of Tammany. He was elevated to the Appellate Division of the
Supreme Court in 1925. By the next year he was ready to return to elective politics and was nominated for the United
States Senate. He told the state convention bestowing the
nomination that it was "the most glorious moment of my life."

☐   Like Wagner, Al Smith worked to reform government
and society, particularly in the aftermath of the Triangle
shirtwaist factory fire of 1911, which killed 146 workers, 123

45

of them girls and young women. But, also like Wagner, Smith did what Murphy needed done to sustain Tammany rule, including playing an instrumental role in the impeachment and removal from office in 1913 of the apostate Governor William Sulzer, who had refused Tammany its patronage. (The impeachment left Wagner as the state's lieutenant governor for a bit more than a year.)

Smith also looked out for himself. In 1915 he received the Democratic nomination for sheriff of New York County. Perhaps the most lucrative public office of the time, the sheriff drew his pay as fees, many of them from the sale of seized items. The take was about $65,000 annually, or the equivalent of more than $1 million per year today. Just as Smith was on the verge of election, however, the legislature was considering a bill that would instead provide the sheriff with a salary—of $12,000 per year, a prospective 80 percent pay cut. Smith used all his influence, with both parties and in both houses, to delay passage of the legislation for two years, long enough for him to change his fortunes. The day after his election as sheriff he began building an extension on his home. That accomplished, he moved on, in 1917, to less remunerative but more prominent service as president of the New York City Board of Aldermen.

For a plain-speaking Irishman, as Oscar Handlin wrote, "up from the city streets," that was as far as he could be expected to go. But Smith was much more sophisticated than he seemed, at least politically. And he was as ambitious as anyone.

Smith's trademark allusions to the world of "The Sidewalks of New York" (the tune was his political anthem) began as genuine but were maintained for image purposes, drawing on a lifelong love for the stage. As Smith adviser (and Crater Supreme Court predecessor) Joseph Proskauer wrote, "The raucous voice and the brown derby were theatrical accessories. The mispronunciation that sometimes made it 'raddio' instead of 'radio' and 'orspital' instead of 'hospital' was born of this theatrical sense." Smith tended the image carefully. When Proskauer sent him a speech draft that included quotes from Franklin, Jefferson, and de Tocqueville, Smith rejected it, sending word: "I'm supposed to know Benjamin Franklin. I'm supposed to know Thomas Jefferson. But if I had ever used that quotation from that French——, everyone would know that Al Smith never wrote that message."

In 1918, Charles Murphy initially favored a gubernatorial nominee from upstate and looked toward Franklin Roosevelt, then serving in Washington as assistant secretary of the navy. But FDR, already holding a national office previously occupied by his wife's uncle Theodore, and with his own sights fixed on following TR's example of attaining an even higher federal post, deferred to Smith. Just as Wagner was fleeing politics for the bench, Smith won the election, defeating incumbent Governor Charles Whitman.

Once in office, Smith became the darling of good-government types. He assembled a very able team around him, including Proskauer, reform activist Belle Moskowitz, and, a bit later, young administrator Robert Moses. They moved to reorganize the state government, painstakingly shifting power from a legislature dominated by upstate interests to the governor. One historian called it "the most thorough renovation of a state government the nation had seen until then." And it was the sort of reform that did nothing to threaten Tammany.

One enemy Smith did make was William Randolph Hearst. Smith had opposed Hearst for mayor in 1905 and for governor in 1906. In 1919, in Smith's first year as governor, a scandal erupted involving bribery aimed at covering up impurities in New York City's milk supply. Smith may not have moved as swiftly or forcefully as he might have against the graft, but he was certainly no defender of, or apologist for, impure milk for city children. Yet that is precisely how Hearst and the Hearst papers portrayed him. The attacks were repeated and vicious, presenting a fine but clear distinction between Smith's populism and Hearst's demagoguery. And they stung.

Finally Governor Smith challenged publisher Hearst to a public debate on the subject at Carnegie Hall. When Hearst declined, Smith appeared anyway, and literally debated an empty chair. The evening was a triumph for Smith, an important marker on his road to statesmanship. "It seems that in every political contest in which I take part," Smith said, "I am called upon to wage the real fight against the figure of Hearst and all that he stands for."

But not even Smith's victory in the milk battle was enough to save him from the landslide of 1920 that placed Warren Harding in the White House. Smith ran more than a million votes ahead of the national Democratic ticket (which included FDR as vice-presidential nominee) as Harding carried even Charles Murphy's "gas house" district. But Smith's bid for a second term as governor fell just short. The *New York Times* recognized that even coming close was noteworthy: "Governor Smith, defeated, has achieved an extraordinary personal and political triumph." He took a lucrative job as chief executive of the U.S. Trucking Company, but with the New York governorship only a two-year term, it was clear that Smith would seek a comeback of some sort in 1922.

In the process, Smith managed to settle one final score with Hearst, and to begin to transcend Tammany itself. The state Democratic convention met in Syracuse in late September 1922. Smith was the likely choice for governor, but Hearst seemed to have secured the nomination for United States senator, with the strong support of New York Mayor John "Red Mike" Hylan and Murphy's at least tacit consent.

But Smith balked. He wanted to be governor again—but, even more than that, he simply would not run on a ticket with Hearst. One historian wrote:

> All that night, the delegates wrestled, not with their consciences, but with their ambitions. The initial shock of the realization that Smith was standing on principle had passed, and their early chagrin had turned to fear. Hearst could never win without Smith on the ticket, the politicians began to realize. Yet Smith might well win alone.

Smith prevailed, both in the convention and at the polls. He was back in the governor's mansion in Albany, and Hearst was no longer, after twenty years, a real force in New York Democratic politics. As a contemporary biographer observed, "It was out of this struggle that the new Smith emerged to discard, figuratively speaking, the brown derby that for so long had adorned the side of his head. He had proved himself, and he knew it, bigger than Tammany. . . ."

Thus unencumbered and emboldened, Smith set out to capture the ultimate prize in American politics, the one office that had always been beyond Tammany's reach: the presidency. At the 1924 Democratic National Convention in New

York's Madison Square Garden, his name was placed in nomination by Franklin Roosevelt. It was Roosevelt's first major
public appearance since being struck by polio three years earlier. In his nominating speech, drafted by Joseph Proskauer,
FDR referred to Smith as the "Happy Warrior." But it was a
very unhappy convention, endlessly deadlocked between
Smith and William Gibbs McAdoo of California, former
president Woodrow Wilson's son-in-law. Only on the 103rd
ballot did an exhausted party, its chances of victory in November already in tatters, turn to the West Virginia native
and New York corporate lawyer John W. Davis.

No one took Davis for a real force in the party. Charles
Murphy had died just months earlier. In an indiscreet mo-
ment, Al Smith told the convention, "I am the leader of the
Democracy in New York."

In 1925, Smith moved to consolidate his control by over-
riding the preferences of the nominal Tammany leader
George Olvany and replacing "Red Mike" Hylan as mayor
with Jimmy Walker. In 1926, Smith rolled to election to a
fourth two-year term as governor by a plurality of more than
a quarter of a million votes. The *New York Times* declared
that "Alfred E. Smith today is the most powerful leader the
Democratic Party has ever had in the greatest State of the
Union." He and others began to call their organization the
"New Tammany."

In fact it was Al Smith himself who was changing, becoming much more a pillar of the society he sought to lead
than an organization loyalist-cum-reformer. Beginning in
1923 he had accepted cash gifts of $143,000 (about $1.5 million today) as well as stock options later worth $250,000
(more than $2.6 million today) over five years from Wall

Street lawyer Thomas Chadbourne. He let lapse the lease on the family homestead on Oliver Street, not far from the Brooklyn Bridge, and lived with his family, when in New York City, at the posh Hotel Biltmore. He took up golf. The public continued to call him "Al," but fewer and fewer people used his first name to his face.

In 1928, Alfred E. Smith reached the pinnacle of his power—only to have it shatter in disillusion. It was his Icarus moment. He was nominated for president by the Democrats, the first Catholic ever to receive a major party nomination for that office (and the last for thirty-two years). But when he was soundly defeated by Herbert Hoover in November, Smith largely ignored the effects that general prosperity and the issue of prohibition had had on the vote (he was a staunch "wet" and, on Murphy's direct order, had in 1923 signed the repeal of New York's "Baby Volstead Act," the Mullan–Gage Act).

Instead he focused on the anti-Catholic bias that had prevailed in the campaign. Privately he complained, "The time hasn't come when a man can say his beads in the White House." The fact that he had not even carried the state of New York, even as Franklin Roosevelt was being elected to succeed him as governor, only made the sting sharper. With the turn of the year 1929, Smith found himself out of office and angry with his countrymen. Having cut himself adrift from Tammany, which largely sat on its hands in the 1928 campaign, and now shorn of the power base of the governorship, Smith found that almost overnight he had gone from "leader of the Democracy in New York" to chief executive of the rising Empire State Building. He was well off in the boom year of 1929—his Empire State salary was five times what he had received as governor, and John J. Raskob, of du Pont and

General Motors, made him a gift of $139,000 (another $1.5 million today) to augment the fortune he had earlier received from Chadbourne. But he was also well out of sorts.

Many observers believed that Al Smith was done in politics. Smith was not so sure; his autobiography, published in 1929, was entitled *Up to Now*. But Smith was at odds with the mayor of New York, Jimmy Walker, and with the new governor, Roosevelt, over their evident desires to assert their own independence from him. FDR was laying the groundwork for a presidential campaign of his own. When the stock market crashed just seven months into Herbert Hoover's term, it began to appear that the Democratic nomination in 1932 could be worth much more than it had been in 1928. Walker, in early 1929, engineered the replacement of George Olvany as Tammany leader with John Curry. Curry declared, "It is a fiction, the New Tammany. I will carry out the policies in which I grew up."

☐ James J. Walker, the mayor Al Smith installed in City Hall, had grown up in the same milieu as John Curry. But Walker was a man of contradictions.

He seemed to be a carefree, debonair gent, the blithe "Night Mayor of New York," the very embodiment of Gotham in the Roaring Twenties. A self-proclaimed "critical" analysis, published in 1927, called him "the most charming Mayor in the history of New York City." Another reporter wrote that "New York wore James J. Walker in its lapel, and he returned the compliment." He was impeccably groomed, elaborately clothed, well—even excessively—rested, apparently above the fray. But things in Walker's world were often not as they seemed.

As corruption in the municipal courts began to surface in the early summer of 1930, Mayor Walker appeared unaffected. Just four weeks before Crater's disappearance, the *New York Times*, which had never been greatly impressed by Jimmy Walker, but had almost always been charmed by him, suggested that "The hour has come for the mayor to summon both the demolition and reconstruction crews. . . . It is not too late for Mr. Walker, who has in no personal way been even slightly connected with any of these scandals, to voice the indignation of the community which has twice elected him."

Of course, it wasn't so simple for Walker. The connections *were* personal, and they weren't slight. Indeed, they went back a full generation. James Walker was born in Greenwich Village in 1881. (He selected his own middle name, John, at the time of his confirmation.) His father William, known to all as Billy, was forty-one years old when his son was born, an immigrant from Castlecomer, in Ireland's County Kilkenny. The elder Walker was active in the Tammany machine and, beginning when young Jim was five years old, served four terms on the city's Board of Aldermen. Following that he was elected to one term in the State Assembly and then appointed Superintendent of Public Buildings. For him, the objects of politics were entirely local: he pointed with pride to a cemetery converted into a park, and to a new recreational pier.

In 1901–1902, Billy Walker became embroiled in a fight within Tammany between would-be reformers, whom Walker supported, and the forces of the fading boss Richard Croker. In 1902, when Walker stood for nomination for the party leadership in his former Assembly district, he encountered a bitter and expensive campaign and was defeated. His finances depleted, he did not, however, retreat from politics altogether, finding a place on the senior staff of Manhattan borough president John Ahearn.

After a reform group called the Citizens Union alleged corruption in Ahearn's office, including kickbacks on building contracts, the borough president asked a number of key lieutenants to resign, among them Billy Walker. Walker protested but complied. Ahearn himself was then called to Albany for hearings on his conduct before Governor Charles Evans Hughes. When the hearings ended, Hughes ordered the removal from office of Ahearn and Bronx borough president Louis Haffen—the first time in history that a governor had ousted elected city leaders. The entire experience was a humiliation for Billy Walker, and almost certainly as well for his son James, now twenty-five years old. The elder Walker sued for reinstatement to his post, and won, but then resigned again, saying that he had brought the suit only to clear his name. His political career was at an end.

His son, meanwhile, seemed to have no interest in civic affairs. He was, instead, an aspiring songwriter. In 1908 he collaborated with musician Ernest Ball and penned the lyrics to his only significant hit, "Will You Love Me in December as You Did in May?" The chorus asked,

> *Will you love me in December as you do in May?*
> *Will you love me in the same old-fashioned way?*
> *When my hair has turned to gray, Will you kiss me then and say*
> *That you love me in December as you did in May?*

Whatever the limitations of the song, it was an immediate smash hit, and for the rest of his life people played it enthusiastically wherever Jimmy Walker went.

54

Where he went next was into politics, almost certainly lured by the secure employment prospects it offered to a loyal Tammany man. And perhaps having learned a lesson from his father, loyal he certainly was. In 1909, just fifteen months after his big song's publication, Walker was elected to the State Assembly, following in Billy's footsteps. After five years he moved on to the State Senate, making his name there by leading populist battles to legalize Sunday baseball and to permit boxing matches to be decided after fifteen rounds. Introduced to Albany by Al Smith, he succeeded Robert Wagner as the Democrats' leader in the Senate and soon signed on Wagner's niece as his personal secretary.

It was in the legislature that Jimmy Walker came into his own. Al Smith said, "This boy is a greater strategist than General Sheridan and he rides twice as fast." His songwriting had been a harbinger of his natural leanings—he was a showman. Thus, finding himself stymied in the legislative session of 1923–1924, despite a nominal one-vote majority in the Senate, Walker one night summoned the only missing member of his caucus to Albany from a Brooklyn sickbed. The lieutenant governor was absent, which made majority leader Walker president pro tem. In this capacity he invoked a rule that barred members from leaving the chamber without his permission, hung a weight on the chamber's large upright clock to prevent it from advancing beyond midnight (when the rules would have required adjournment), and brought the entire Democratic legislative program up for votes, ramming one bill after another home to passage. When first the Senate clerk and then the deputy clerk went hoarse marching through the required readings of bills, Walker took the rostrum to complete the work himself.

On another occasion, Walker had just orchestrated the passage of a bill, only to see his Republican counterpart scurrying around the chamber and appearing to be on the verge of assembling sufficient votes to force reconsideration of the measure. Walker privately approached the Senate clerk and asked that the bill just passed be certified and transmitted to the Assembly, not at the end of the day's session but right at that moment. The clerk hesitated but soon succumbed to Walker's invocation of a little-known Senate rule giving party leaders the right to obtain immediate certification. When the Republican leader rose, votes for reconsideration in hand, Walker calmly asked, "Is the bill still at the desk?" As he knew, technically it was not.

Walker was witty, and quick, and, unlike many politicians, was not afraid to deploy these talents in debate. On one occasion he demolished an anti-pornography measure pending before the legislature, known as the "Clean Books" bill, with the quip, "Why all this talk about womanhood? I have never yet heard of a girl being ruined by a book."

He was Tammany's man, and in 1925, with a strong assist from Bronx boss Ed Flynn, the machine made him mayor, replacing the inept "Red Mike" Hylan. The mayoral oath of office was administered to Walker by Justice Robert Wagner. Walker brought bounce to his new job, and style, but little substance. He told a group of City Hall reporters, "I've read not more than fifteen books cover to cover. . . . What little I know, I have learned by ear." And it was not false modesty—he meant it.

But he was never above having fun, especially when it could be had at the expense of those who took public affairs more seriously. He described a reformer as "a guy who rides through a sewer in a glass-bottomed boat." When a representative of the group that had driven his father from office rose to testify at a Board of Estimate meeting, the mayor asked him to state his affiliation:

> "Citizens Union," replied the man.
> "Did you say Citizen Union?" queried Jimmy.
> "The *Citizens* Union," corrected the nettled reformer.
> "Aha," exclaimed Walker, "then there are two of you."

He applied himself diligently to his new job until he grew bored with the work of the mayoralty, which seemed to take about six weeks. Thereafter he came into City Hall at three o'clock in the afternoon—when he came in at all. In his first two years in office, 1926 and 1927, he took seven vacations for a total of 143 days, or ten weeks of vacation a year. He visited Atlanta, Houston, and San Francisco, attended the Kentucky Derby, and went abroad not only to Canada and Cuba but to London, Paris, Berlin, and Rome. (By contrast, Al Smith, eight years older than Walker, had never been outside the country at the time he ran for president in 1928.)

And when in New York, Walker pampered himself. At home, according to a contemporary account, he wore "gorgeous dressing gowns and pajamas. The dressing gowns are all tight-waisted and flaring below the waistline. With the fringed sash that is part of them, and the rich colors of which their pattern is composed, he gives the impression of some exotic Oriental as he walks in some sort of stealthy, half-military manner around the room."

Nor was the attention to detail in his appearance confined to home. He never wore anything to City Hall except a business suit, invariably a dark one, except in summer when he

57

adopted lighter shades. Indeed, he designed his own clothes and had them custom-made by an Austrian tailor. His suits, were, according to chroniclers of the day, "extremely form-fitting, and the break in the waist-line must be just so. The back of the coat is straight across, the sleeves taper and are about an inch narrower at the wrists than in coats other men wear. The breast pocket on the outside of the coat is not slightly aslant but straight across and the vest has seven buttons instead of the conventional six. The trousers are without cuffs, but he is fond of cuffs on sleeves and of lapels on the vest. In this he is practical. He believes that cuffs are ornaments but that on pants they are only dust-gatherers."

But practicality was not the objective. The objective was to stand out: "His favorite combination consists of three shades of the same solid color; as a blue suit, a lighter blue tie and a lighter or darker blue shirt. With such an outfit he will wear a gray soft hat and dark shoes. A ring worn on the little finger forms a part of his dressing scheme. He changes it so that the stone matches his clothes, and it must also match the cuff links."

As Walker summed up his own credo, "There are a lot of things in life that we cannot do anything about, but a man's beard is his own fault."

For all this evident clamoring for attention, however, Walker disliked actually being touched by strangers. He feared crowds, insisting on standing with his back to a pillar at football games and waiting until the crowd had departed before he would leave. His wife later recalled that he "couldn't stand being mauled, and very much disliked being slapped on the back or having anyone grab hold of his lapels." He seems to have been claustrophobic in elevators.

And the man who came, for many, to represent New York City in the Jazz Age, refused to learn to drive a car—or to permit his chauffeur to go faster than twenty miles per hour or to disobey a single traffic regulation. Seemingly without a care in the world, he suffered from a chronically nervous stomach, consistently cold and clammy hands, and frequent night sweats.

Walker had met the showgirl Janet "Allie" Allen in 1904, and they had become involved almost immediately, but it was more than seven years before they married and she moved into his parents' home, by which time Jimmy was already in politics. He was two hours late for the wedding. His infidelities were frequent and may well have begun even before the couple married. Years later, Allie recalled that

> We were always happy together. If I felt neglected or left out, I never tried to show it, and always cooperated with Jim in anything or any way that would be for his benefit. We never quarreled, and when I talked to him about situations that made me uncomfortable and unhappy, he always said that it was a passing phase, and no one would ever take my place. And I believed him.

This remained the state of Walker's affairs while Charles Murphy controlled Tammany Hall. Murphy acted as a brake on Walker, and the party leader had ambitions for the young man, beyond the Senate leadership in which he had already installed him. When Murphy named Walker to his Senate post, Walker asked, "What about patronage?" Murphy replied, "Use your own judgment. If it's good, you'll be an asset to the party. If it isn't—well, the sooner we find out, the better."

Had Murphy succeeded in securing the Democratic presidential nomination for Al Smith in 1924, there was talk that Walker would have been the Tammany candidate for governor that year. But Murphy died suddenly some months before the 1924 convention, and Smith failed to get the party nod for president. Walker's discretion continued, but not for much longer.

He had begun a long-running affair in 1917 with a dancer named Yvonne "Vonnie" Shelton, an orphan who had been involved with a string of older men since coming to New York as a teenager. She was introduced to Walker by reform mayor John Purroy Mitchel. Now, with Murphy dead, the Walker–Shelton affair became more open and notorious. Governor Smith, always somewhat puritanical, was outraged and ordered Walker to return to his wife, on pain of losing the 1925 mayoral nomination that seemed likely to come his way. At first Walker—who loved to tweak Smith by calling him "Algie," a nickname Smith despised—simply became more discreet, but finally, with the election approaching, and after a visit to Miss Shelton by representatives of Tammany, Walker broke off the eight-year relationship and made a great public show of marital fidelity.

Such discipline did not come naturally to Walker. A pair of lobbyists, seeking to write each other in a private cipher, code-named Walker "Boy Friend." In the first year of his mayoralty he began another affair with another showgirl, this one named Betty Compton. She was twenty-two, and had been acting since she was seven years old; she had married at eighteen and divorced within a year. Two years after Walker met her, he moved out on his wife and began appearing everywhere with Compton, frequently literally dancing until dawn.

By 1929 the act was beginning to wear thin with some.

As the good times rolled to an end, Walker's salary was raised to $40,000 annually—a 60 percent increase. The raise was put through only after Walker had been reelected and just weeks inside the legal deadline for having it take effect for his second term. It came despite the stock market crash, which had occurred two months earlier. Walker needed the money, to support not only himself, but his estranged wife, who racked up more than $20,000 in charges (more than $200,000 today) at a single clothes shop in two and a half years.

Walker easily defeated Fiorello La Guardia in his bid for reelection, but he was then summoned to the residence of His Eminence Patrick Cardinal Hayes on Madison Avenue, where he was rebuked for his adultery.

Even before the 1929 election, the *New York Times* was talking about unfulfilled potential. Calling Walker witty, quick, alert, brilliant, skillful, and gifted, it nevertheless yearned, as one editorial was titled, for "The Mayor He Might Be":

> What has been lacking . . . has been the steady application of uncommon abilities to the uncommonly complicated and arduous work of the office. The city has stood by and has seen, as it were, great powers going to waste. Citizens have not so much minded Mr. Walker's frequent absences, or his obvious delight in the social side of life, but they have regretted that he has not devoted himself more exclusively and sternly to the big job placed in his hands.

Chapter Three

THE LA GUARDIA
PHENOMENON

☐ Walker's most insistent opponent was Congressman Fiorello H. La Guardia, whose saga was already a remarkable one.

La Guardia was the same age as Governor Roosevelt, just a year younger than Walker, and born, just as Walker had been, in Greenwich Village. But while Walker had spent nearly his entire life in and around New York, La Guardia had truly seen the world. His father, Achille, had been a band leader in the U.S. army since his eldest son was three years old, and young Fiorello (literally, "Little Flower") had spent much of the second decade of his life at the army's Whipple Barracks in desolate Prescott, Arizona, then still a territory rather than a state.

Fiorello was a one-man exemplar of the American melting pot, "a balanced ticket all by himself." His mother Irene, *nee* Luzzato Coen, was a practicing Jew of Italian extraction. Achille, raised a Catholic, at the time of his marriage gave his religion as "*nessuno*," "nothing." But their son Americanized his multiple given middle names Rafael Enrico to the simple "Henry," sometimes identified himself as an Episcopalian, and did not even learn Italian until he was twenty years old, and then for professional purposes. He mastered and deployed his mother's Yiddish for similar reasons. At thirty he became a Freemason, and later told a biographer, "Free Masonry is my religion. A man who could live up to the teachings of the Order would do no other."

The Spanish-American War changed Fiorello's life, even though he didn't get to join the fight. His father was ordered to Mobile, Alabama, and then to Tampa, Florida, en route to entertain U.S. troops in Cuba. Fiorello, just sixteen years old and calling himself "Frank," had wangled a job as a correspondent for the *St. Louis Post-Dispatch*; he joined Achille in Mobile. But the elder La Guardia ate "embalmed beef" provided to the army by a shoddy contractor, which left him with hepatitis, soon complicated by malaria. Instead of sharing the glory of Theodore Roosevelt's Rough Riders, Achille was soon honorably discharged with "diseases of the stomach and bowels, catarrh of the throat and head and malarial poisoning." After thirteen years of service, this earned him a pension of $8 per month, roughly $2,000 annually in today's currency. His health would never entirely recover, and he was disgusted with America. Like the Wagners, the La Guardia family quit the New World, moving back to Italy, and joined Irene's mother in Trieste for the last six years of Achille's life.

Fiorello was forever enraged by what had happened to his father, and especially by the corruption that he believed had made it possible. But he did not share Achille's disillusionment with America. He escaped Italy by joining the U.S. foreign service and served in consulates in Budapest and Fiume for five years beginning when he was nineteen.

Fiorello then returned to America after an eight-year absence and took jobs in Ohio and New York before establishing himself permanently in New York in 1907. He had never graduated from high school or college, but he took to studying law at night, using his unusual facility with languages to become an interpreter of Croatian, Italian, and German on Ellis Island, where the immigrant wave was near its peak. He was earning $1,200 per year, nearly $22,500 today.

But nothing could hold La Guardia's attention for long. Although he became a lawyer, politics was already his passion. Seeing little opportunity for someone named La Guardia in the Irish world of Tammany, he joined a Republican club and entered a subscription for the *Congressional Record*, which he devoured.

His instincts tended toward reform, but when that clashed with his ambition, ambition often prevailed. In 1912 he refused to join TR's insurgency within the Republican party against TR's successor, William Howard Taft. Just when young Franklin Roosevelt was championing the reform candidacy of Woodrow Wilson, La Guardia took pride in "being regular in every sense of the word." It earned him a place as Republican district captain. The next year La Guardia stuck with the Republicans rather than support the Fusion mayoral effort of John Purroy Mitchel.

La Guardia had long wanted to run for something himself, and he got the chance in 1914. One summer evening at the local clubhouse, the Republican nomination for Congress in the Fourteenth District, a Tammany bastion, was going begging. What occurred that evening was fictionalized in Sheldon Harnick's lyrics to the song "Politics and Poker" in the musical *Fiorello!*—*Gentlemen, how about some names we can use? Some qualified Republican who's willing to lose.* But not fictionalized by much. "I'll take it," La Guardia said. One club member urged the selection of "someone whose name we can spell," but La Guardia prevailed. Nonetheless, his biographer notes, "he was listed as 'Floullo' on the official manual of candidates for the State."

He waged a spirited campaign, speaking Italian in Italian neighborhoods, Yiddish to Jews, and working constantly. He wore a black Stetson and string tie evocative of his Arizona boyhood. "To look at his heavy, round, jowly face, one would think that his voice would be deep and perhaps resonant. It was neither and sounded like an older choir boy's tenor-alto."

And he came remarkably close to winning—close enough to earn a patronage appointment as a deputy attorney general in preparation for another run in 1916. When Republican bosses moved instead to give the 1916 nomination to Hamilton Fish, Jr., who later served twelve terms in the House from upstate New York, La Guardia threatened a primary and Fish backed down. This time La Guardia was elected, by all of 357 votes. He was the first Italian-American in Congress, and the first Republican elected from the Fourteenth District.

La Guardia took office early in 1917. Within months America had entered the Great War. In July, Representative La Guardia, ever eager for action, enlisted as a lieutenant in the army's aviation section. But this was not just for show. By October he had been promoted to captain and shipped off to Foggia, Italy. He gained his flight certification in December and soon crashed a plane, suffering a permanently debilitating back injury. According to his biographer, "His flying technique was still pure hands and glands. 'I can't take the buzzard off and I can't land him,' he told one of his men, 'but I can fly the son of a gun.'" By August 1918 he was a major, and for the rest of his life that was his favorite title.

Returning from the war, and to his congressional seat, La Guardia married Thea Almerigotti, a devout Catholic, in 1919. Later that same year, with the mayoralty of New York in his sights, he was elected president of the city Board of Aldermen—the same job Al Smith had left to become governor—and resigned from the Congress. His election to the presidency of the Board of Aldermen was the first time a Republican-line-only candidate had won citywide office since the merger of New York and Brooklyn in 1898.

In June 1920, Fiorello and Thea had a baby they named Fioretta Thea. But tragedy then derailed not only La Guardia's career but his life. Both mother and daughter were tubercular. La Guardia moved his family from Greenwich Village to the more healthful Bronx, then rented a home on Long Island for his wife while placing his infant daughter in the hospital. Soon he again uprooted Thea, packing her off to a sanitarium in Saranac Lake, New York. In May 1921, during a year in which he had intended to devote all his energies to running for mayor, La Guardia instead buried his eleven-month-old only child; six months later his wife died as well. The marriage had lasted two and a half years.

La Guardia had run for the Republican mayoral nomination anyway, in the midst of this personal disaster, but it was his least effective and least successful campaign. In 1922, out of office and newly widowed, he plotted a comeback. His aim again was the House of Representatives, but this time from a different seat, the Republican Twentieth District, much of it located in East Harlem.

His Tammany opponent was Henry Frank, a Jewish attorney. Frank and his Tammany supporters immediately sought to draw the battle along ethnic lines, accusing La Guardia of anti-Semitism and of being a "Jew hater." Frank, they noted, was "a Jew with a Jewish heart, and who does good for us." La Guardia lashed back in an "open letter" to Frank, which he had printed up in Yiddish. It contained a challenge to Frank to "publicly and openly debate the issues of the campaign, THE DEBATE TO BE CONDUCTED BY YOU AND ME *ENTIRELY IN THE YIDDISH LANGUAGE.*"

Frank, as La Guardia well knew, did not speak Yiddish.

Frank nevertheless won the Jewish parts of the district handily, but La Guardia did the same in the Italian neighborhoods. When all of the votes were counted and recounted, La Guardia was back in Congress—by a margin of eleven votes.

Many politicians in such a situation would move smartly to the middle of the spectrum. Not La Guardia. Back in the House, he now broke almost completely with the Harding and then Coolidge administrations. In 1924 he refused a Republican nomination he would probably have been denied in any event, and successfully sought reelection from

East Harlem as a Socialist, while supporting Progressive nominee Robert La Follette for president. Just six years earlier he had challenged the patriotism of his Socialist opponent, saying that "the Socialist Party doesn't pretend to be 100 per cent loyal." But now he needed whatever support he could muster, and that of the Socialists was sufficient to secure him a 40 percent plurality in a three-candidate field. The La Guardia campaign was directed by personal loyalists who called themselves the "Ghibboni" (literally "apes," but colloquially something akin to "swashbucklers"). The most outstanding figure in this crowd was a twenty-two-year-old named Vito Marcantonio, much later a literally Communist-leaning member of Congress. Marcantonio soon moved into La Guardia's Bronx home.

In the mid-twenties, La Guardia's independence and theatricality—one journalist dubbed him "the Belasco of politics"—earned him increasing citywide, and even national attention. In these years the *New York Times* was chronicling his exploits about once a week; by 1928 the articles were coming nearly every other day. While Jimmy Walker saw the glass of the Jazz Age as three-quarters full, Fiorello La Guardia relentlessly saw it as one-quarter empty.

In 1926, to dramatize what he considered the absurdity of prohibition, La Guardia called a press conference in a House office building and publicly mixed two legal drinks, "near beer" and malt extract, to create 2 percent beer, a prohibited beverage. Challenged to repeat the stunt without the cloak of official immunity provided by the House building, he called another press conference, this one at Kaufman's pharmacy on Lenox Avenue in Harlem, and did it again.

The next year he took on the meat industry, which he still held responsible for his father's misfortune, on charges of price gouging. Turning for help to the secretary of agriculture, La Guardia was directed to a pamphlet on the economical uses of meat. When the Department of Agriculture's appropriations bill came to the floor of the House, Congressman La Guardia took his revenge. He waved around another USDA pamphlet, this one on "Lamb and Mutton and Their Uses in the Diet," and reminded his colleagues that "90 percent of the people of New York City cannot afford to eat lamb chops." Then he pulled such a chop from his vest pocket, a steak from another pocket and a roast from yet another. "The issue was not how to make economical use of meat but how to get meat. 'Gentlemen, we simply have to eat. We have formed the habit.' "

But he did not confine himself to stunts. Just as he had not simply marched off to war but had put himself at genuine risk in combat, so, when a pistol-waving lunatic threatened the House from the gallery, La Guardia ran to tackle the man. And the courage could be moral as well as physical. When Oscar De Priest came to Washington as the first black in the House in the twentieth century and many of his colleagues sought to ostracize him, La Guardia volunteered to be placed next to him.

Yet, just when La Guardia seemed comprehensible as a principled reformer, he could surprise again. Once a Hearst ally, he broke with the publisher rather than mount a hopeless challenge to Walker's first campaign for mayor in 1925. In the Sixty-ninth Congress of 1925–1926 he had been the Socialist whip, or deputy floor leader. But faced

with a tough reelection battle in 1926, he deserted the Socialists and returned to the Republican fold, enabling him
to pull out a fifty-vote victory in another three-way campaign. He was not even above a bit of vote-rigging himself.
One young supporter recalled his rationalization this way:
"We must fight fire with fire—all is fair in love, war, and
politics. They are stealing, cheating, and murdering us,
and we must fight them on their own grounds. . . . He was
better than Tammany and he had to win."

"Fiorello La Guardia," a recent biographer noted, "was,
first and foremost, a professional pol—though God help any
man who so defined him to his face!" In 1929 the Republicans finally named La Guardia to run for mayor as Walker
sought reelection. In this campaign La Guardia attempted to
mix his advocacy of reform with appeals to ethnics—one of
his campaign songs declared, "He's proud he's an American/
And he's proud he's a Wop"—and he refused to renounce the
support of American fascists.

As the mayor floated above his attacks, La Guardia grew
nearly hysterical. He made not-so-veiled references to
Walker's philandering (La Guardia had married his own
longtime secretary and political lieutenant, Marie Fisher, in
February 1929). He called for the voters to "Elect a full time
Mayor, who will sleep at night and work in the daytime." He
made numerous accusations of corruption, many of them
quite specific.

It made no difference. Even with the election coming a
week after the stock market crash, he lost by nearly half a
million votes, pulling just 26 percent of the total. Just nine
months before Joseph Crater disappeared, Fiorello La
Guardia suffered the greatest defeat, and Jimmy Walker won

the greatest victory of any major party mayoral candidate in the modern history of the city of New York. Walker told his police commissioner that "this election proves that a man can wear his own clothes."

☐   But just as there are no final victories in politics, La Guardia repeatedly demonstrated that defeats are also often not final. This was especially true of his 1929 campaign.

One of the most specific of La Guardia's 1929 charges had involved two men whose fall would provide a significant element of the backdrop to the disappearance of Judge Crater. Magistrate Albert Vitale, La Guardia alleged, had "borrowed" $20,000 from Arnold Rothstein.

Arnold Rothstein was a vertically integrated gambler—that is, he both placed wagers and acted as a bookmaker. On occasion he was also known to take steps to affect the outcome of events on which he had money riding. One such occasion was the 1919 World Series, in which Rothstein bankrolled payments to members of the Chicago White Sox (later recalled as the "Black Sox") for losing to the underdog Cincinnati Reds. As Jay Gatsby explained to Nick Carroway, "He just saw the opportunity." (Rothstein later denied involvement, saying "cheap gamblers" had "used my name to put it over.")

Rothstein was a protégé of Big Tim Sullivan, Tammany leader of the Bowery and Tenderloin districts in the early years of the twentieth century. Tammany had long enjoyed a close relationship with elements of the underworld. As Herbert Asbury put it, "The political geniuses of Tammany Hall were quick to see the practical value of the gangsters, and to realize the advisability of providing them with meeting and hiding places, that their favor might be curried, and their peculiar talents employed on election day to assure government of, by, and for Tammany."

When the leading gangster Herman Rosenthal was murdered in 1912, and with Big Tim in declining health, Rothstein, then just thirty years old, became the key link in this chain.

> Over the next few years, Rothstein provided all manner of services for [Tammany]—hiring hoodlums to stuff ballot boxes, posting bail bonds for the unlucky, serving as a bag man for the gathering of tribute. Similarly, Arnold handled the fixing of nightclub violations, the granting of boxing licenses, the evasion of laws and ordinances great and small. In each instance, he took his cut. While he was still in his thirties, his fortune had grown to half a million dollars [or nearly $9 million today].

Thus established, he branched out in the 1920s into stock-dumping "bucket shops," bootlegging, and drugs.

He also became somewhat more discreet. In his book *Gangs of New York*, published in 1928, Asbury observed that "there are now no gangs in New York, and no gangsters in the sense that the word has come into common use. In his day the gangster flourished under the protection and manipulation of the crooked politician to whom he was an invaluable ally at election time, but his day has simply passed."

Rothstein's was, of course, a dangerous business, and he met a messy end. On Sunday evening, November 4, 1928, he was summoned from his usual table at Lindy's restaurant to Room 349 of the nearby Park Central Hotel. Waiting for him there was likely George McManus, another gambler, who had organized a three-day gambling marathon, perhaps fixed, in which Rothstein had recently lost $322,000. (It was quite a card game—the sum equates to more than $3.3 million today.) McManus wanted Rothstein to pay; Rothstein refused. Perhaps after taunting a drunken McManus, Rothstein was shot in the abdomen. He stumbled down the back stairs, sought to hail a taxi, and collapsed. The gun that had been used to shoot him lay nearby on the street, tossed from a hotel window.

Rothstein was taken to Polyclinic Hospital where he lingered nearly thirty-six hours, drifting in and out of consciousness but refusing to identify his attacker. "Got nothing to say," he said. "Nothing, nothing. Won't talk about it." On Tuesday, November 6, as Herbert Hoover was overwhelmingly defeating Al Smith for the presidency and Franklin Roosevelt was narrowly being elected governor, Arnold Rothstein died.

Despite numerous clues pointing to the identity of his assailant—an expensive overcoat with the name "George McManus" embroidered into its lining and handkerchiefs monogrammed "GAM" were found by a maid in the room where the shooting had taken place—the police, under the leadership of Walker's commissioner, Joseph Warren, failed to make an arrest. The case was hugely inconvenient, and no one in the administration was eager for it to be solved.

Warren was suffering from the advanced stages of some disease, probably syphilis, which affected him both mentally and physically, and had for some time. With public pressure mounting to crack the Rothstein murder case, this now became too obvious. Walker removed Warren, who was placed in a sanitarium and soon died. In his place the mayor named as commissioner Grover Whalen, a great showman (his ultimate triumph was the 1939 World's Fair) if not a great lawman.

Even after McManus turned himself in three weeks after the shooting, the indictment was long delayed. But Whalen launched a very public crackdown on petty crime, and the Rothstein case faded from view. McManus was eventually tried for the killing, but no fewer than five witnesses recanted on the stand, and he was acquitted.

In the mayoral campaign of 1929, one of La Guardia's charges was that Magistrate Vitale had borrowed a large sum of money from Rothstein. The implications, La Guardia insisted, were obvious. Vitale heatedly denied the charge and claimed to be a man of integrity. Like everything else in La Guardia's 1929 campaign, no one seemed to notice.

But a few weeks after Walker had been reelected, that changed. On Saturday evening, December 7, 1929, a dinner in Vitale's honor was convened by the Tepecano Democratic Club at the Roman Gardens in the Bronx. Among the guests was Ciro Terranova, the so-called Artichoke King, who held an effective monopoly on the sale of vegetables in Italian-American neighborhoods as well as other less savory business interests. Terranova had been acquitted of two murders and made a practice of riding around town in armor-plated vehicles. Police Commissioner Whalen called him the "Al Capone of New York."

Past midnight, six or seven armed men entered the Roman Gardens, simultaneously drew their weapons, and announced a holdup. Police Detective Arthur Johnson, who had come, he later said, for some "eats," was seated at Magistrate Vitale's left. Johnson turned to the judge, who, he later testified,

> "shook his head at me."
>
> "Did you believe that to be a signal to you?" the patrolman was asked.
>
> "I figured that he meant, 'Don't start anything.'. . ."
>
> "Did you have in mind the safety of the diners?"
>
> "Absolutely."
>
> "Did you feel that if you took any action it might provoke a fusillade of shots?"
>
> "It would have meant a slaughter."

Johnson was immediately relieved of his service revolver, and Vitale's guests were relieved of nearly $5,000 in cash and their jewels. Vitale managed to slip off his diamond ring and hide it in his pants, although he did surrender $40 in cash.

Vitale could not easily hide his embarrassment, but he could make amends, and he did so remarkably quickly. Returning to his political club in the early hours of the morning, Vitale made a few phone calls. Johnson continues the tale:

> Around 4 A.M. Sunday, I was called to the Tepecano Democratic Club and Judge Vitale brought me to an anteroom where there was a desk. . . . He pulled out the top right-hand drawer and said, "There is your gun." I asked him where he had got the gun and he was unable to advise me, stating that it had come back and that was all he knew about it.

The cash and jewelry were similarly returned to the guests. Johnson was suspended and demoted, although Vitale petitioned to have him restored to rank.

But the story was too good for others to ignore. The police tried to point the finger of blame at Terranova, saying that he had staged the heist to retrieve embarrassing documents held by some of the diners. But the Artichoke King insisted that politics had been at the heart of the episode. Noting that Vitale was a protégé of Bronx boss Ed Flynn, a former Al Smith associate who had begun serving as secretary of state for Roosevelt in Albany, Terranova hypothesized that intra-Tammany feuding was at work: "The Walker–Hylan unit, in order to injure Mr. Smith, tried to harm Mr. Flynn. To do that they pick on Vitale, one of Mr. Flynn's supporters. To get Vitale they make a goat out of me."

But it was Vitale who became the goat of the affair. Investigators quickly determined that La Guardia's allegations about Vitale's borrowing from Rothstein had been accurate. Seeking greater profits in the stock market, Vitale had borrowed $19,940 on June 17 or 18, 1928 (more than $200,000 in today's dollars), and had repaid the loan two weeks later to Rothstein's Rothmere Mortgage Corporation. He had given a lawyer serving as his intermediary with Rothstein a signed note with both the payee and amount blank; but he had known of Rothstein and knew that the gambler was the source of the loan. It is not clear what interest rate, if any, Rothstein charged Vitale for this service. It did become clear that Vitale had released a robber friend of Rothstein's from custody, even though the man had been caught redhanded. Soon after the revelations, Vitale was removed from office by the Appellate Division for having "brought [the courts] into a political campaign and involved [them] in a loathsome scandal."

For his part, early in 1930 La Guardia said, "I can say to the people who voted against me last year, 'I told you so.'"

Chapter Four

FRANKLIN
ROOSEVELT
NAMES A JUDGE

☐ The relationship between Franklin Roosevelt, who named Joseph Crater to the bench, and Tammany Hall, from which Crater came, was complicated—and always had been.

Roosevelt had been elected to the New York State Senate in 1910, successful in his first bid for political office, largely on the strength of his wife's uncle Theodore's name—the surname he and Eleanor shared even before their marriage. Franklin was only the second Democrat to represent his senatorial district since the founding of the Republican party. It was only twelve years since TR had been elected governor of New York, less than two years since he had left the White

House, and just months since he had split with his handpicked successor as president, William Howard Taft. While Theodore and Franklin were only fifth cousins, and members of opposing political parties, the Roosevelt name in 1910 was so powerful in New York that it served immediately to put the most junior member of the Senate in the Albany spotlight.

And young Senator Roosevelt used that attention to seize the leadership of a rare intraparty challenge to Tammany. Less than three weeks after he took his seat in the legislature, in January 1911, Roosevelt was the subject of a *New York Times* profile recounting the first impression he had made on his new peers:

> Those who looked closely at the lawmaker behind Desk 26 saw a young man with the finely chiseled face of a Roman patrician, only with the ruddier glow of health on it. Nature has left much unfinished in modeling the face of the Roosevelt of greater fame. On the face of this Roosevelt, younger in years and in public service, she has lavished all her refining processes until much of the elementary strength has been lost in the sculpturing.
>
> Senator Roosevelt is less than thirty [actually, just a week short of 29]. He is tall and lithe. With his handsome face and his form of supple strength he could make a fortune on the stage and set the matinee girl's heart throbbing with subtle and happy emotion. But no one would suspect behind that highly polished exterior the quiet force and determination that now are sending cold shivers down the spine of Tammany's striped mascot.

The battle was immediately joined over the determination of Tammany leader Murphy, boss since 1902, that

William Sheehan would be the next United States senator from New York. U.S. senators were then chosen by the state legislature, and with a newly elected Democratic majority in both houses, Murphy believed he could, and felt entitled to, dictate the choice of Sheehan—"Blue-Eyed Billy," the former Democratic boss of Buffalo. Murphy entrusted the task to his new leaders in Albany, Assembly majority leader Al Smith and State Senate leader Robert Wagner. Young Senator Roosevelt took another view.

The stakes, all saw, were large. If the Democratic wave that had begun to build with the Taft–TR split in 1910 continued to crest, there was a chance that in 1912 the Democrats could win just their third presidential election since the rise of Abraham Lincoln more than half a century earlier. If that happened, the new Democratic U.S. senator would have at his disposal substantial federal patronage—a new supply of lifeblood for Tammany. And for reformers like Franklin Roosevelt, the Senate seat was another skirmish in a brewing fight for control of the national Democratic party itself.

Murphy's endorsement of Sheehan coalesced anti-Tammany feeling upstate and down. Sheehan had been a bitter opponent, in intraparty fights, of the man who in 1884 and 1892 had won those two most recent terms in the White House for the Democrats, Buffalo's own Grover Cleveland. The *New York Times* howled, "It is a monstrous travesty of politics that Charles F. Murphy should have anything whatever to say about the election of a Senator."

Murphy endorsed Sheehan on January 11, 1911. The Democratic caucus of state legislators met five days later to confirm the choice, and Sheehan was duly approved. But twenty-one upstate legislators, sufficient to threaten the nomination with defeat on the floor of the legislature itself, simply refused to attend the meeting. Louis Howe, Albany correspondent of the *New York Herald*, clearly relished the fight: "Never in the history of Albany have 21 men threatened such total ruin of machine plans. It is the most humanly interesting political fight in many years." The leader of the gang of twenty-one so intriguing to Louis Howe was Franklin Roosevelt, a senator now for just over two weeks.

In this fight Roosevelt had a role model, the new governor of New Jersey, Woodrow Wilson, who had succeeded in blocking his own legislature's election of party boss James Smith, Jr. to the U.S. Senate.

The fight over Sheehan raged for nearly three months. The divisions were between reformers and machine adherents, upstaters and down (with the New York City forces pushing for Sheehan), Protestants and Catholics, patricians and strivers. When Smith and Wagner ventured to discuss the matter at the home the Roosevelts were renting in Albany, the butler sniffed, "I know the Senator is expecting Senator Wagner." "That's all right. I'll come along, too," Smith said cheerfully, but he was cut deeply enough that he and his family repeated the story for years. The rent for the home, Roosevelt's fourth residence, was three times Smith's salary.

Murphy had dispatched Wagner and Smith to make sure that Roosevelt was not trying to destroy the machine itself. He assured them that he was not. With that, Murphy came to Albany to see the young upstart for himself. They met on Roosevelt's twenty-ninth birthday. While the meeting was exceedingly polite, the rebel leader refused to give ground.

Murphy's enthusiasm for Sheehan now faded. But the prospective nominee refused to go quietly, and Murphy refused entreaties from Wagner to force Sheehan from the race. As February turned into March, reform Democratic governor John Dix tried to do what Murphy felt he could not. He called on the caucus to choose someone other than Sheehan, but Sheehan turned on his own governor as well. Desperate, Murphy asked Roosevelt to talk to Sheehan himself.

Now it was Sheehan's turn to come to the Roosevelt Albany mansion. The luncheon included both men's wives, and must have been remarkably strained, even by Edwardian standards. Afterward, Roosevelt again made clear that his group of insurgents could not be reconciled to a Sheehan candidacy. A new caucus vote, taken only two days after the Triangle fire claimed 146 lives in New York City, found just twenty-eight votes, out of ninety, for Sheehan; Roosevelt's group continued to stay away.

The last straw was another fire—this one in the Assembly chamber in Albany. It forced the caucus to convene instead in Albany's cramped city hall. Political discomfort was now exacerbated by physical discomfort. Murphy folded.

His new choice was Supreme Court Justice James O'Gorman, a sachem of Tammany. Roosevelt wavered for a day, but then he and his group agreed to go along. Some have argued that by choosing a Tammany man and another Catholic, Murphy prevailed. (He also got to name his own son-in-law to replace O'Gorman on the bench.) But it would be more accurate to say that the battle between the longtime machine leader and the freshman legislator had ended in a draw. With Sheehan supporters having raised the religious issue, Roosevelt had no practical choice but to accept another Catholic. And while O'Gorman's local politics were regular, at the national level he was aligned with reformers such as

Wilson. Roosevelt and Murphy had discovered in their brief meeting that they could do business together.

As a 1931 biography of Roosevelt summed up the matter, "One year in Albany had made Roosevelt nationally known, developed within him a consciousness of power to lead men, and given him a taste for public life which has never left him." Louis Howe, "a newspaperman of uncertain employment, meager income and wretched health," soon left his paper to become Roosevelt's chief political operative. By the summer of 1912, Howe was addressing young Senator Roosevelt as "Beloved and Revered Future President."

The entire messy fight had moreover provided a significant boost to the national movement for the direct election of U.S. senators. When the State Senate reconvened in April 1911, Franklin Roosevelt's motion urging the state's congressional delegation to approve a federal constitutional amendment to that effect passed both houses in Albany. The Seventeenth Amendment passed the U.S. Congress the following May.

Any possibility of damage to Roosevelt's career in New York was saved by a rare blunder by Murphy that helped Roosevelt shift his focus from state to national politics. As the 1912 Democratic National Convention in Baltimore neared, Roosevelt had long since committed himself publicly to Wilson's candidacy, chairing the New Jersey governor's New York campaign—and had broken with cousin Theodore, who was mounting a third-party comeback bid. Murphy favored Champ Clark of Missouri, the preconvention favorite.

With a bit of clever help from Roosevelt, the Clark bandwagon was derailed. On Friday night, June 28, 1912, a convention ballot found Clark with a majority of delegates. With only one past exception, such a milestone had always been a harbinger of a candidate going on to amass two-thirds of the votes—and the party's nomination. On Saturday, June 29,

> Roosevelt got word that the Clark leaders had arranged for two or three hundred Baltimore ward leaders and their henchmen to storm the floor at the evening session. The doorkeepers had been instructed to admit all who wore Clark buttons. Roosevelt had a personal friend who was active in Baltimore politics. He agreed to lend Roosevelt about one hundred of his people. Roosevelt lined up another hundred from New York, supplied them all with Clark buttons and instructed them to enter upon the heels of the Clark crowd. At the appropriate moment the Clark shouters poured into the aisles, unfurling banners and shouting, "We Want Clark." In a few seconds there arose from immediately behind them an equally voluminous cry, "We Want Wilson. We Want Wilson." The attempted Clark stampede disintegrated into pandemonium, verging on a riot. Both brigades were eventually thrown off the floor.

Wilson was nominated on the forty-sixth ballot.

As president, Wilson refused to recognize any role for Murphy and Tammany in the distribution of federal patronage in New York State, and instead consulted Roosevelt and others who had supported him in Baltimore. And Senator Roosevelt became Assistant Secretary of the Navy Roosevelt—the same job cousin Theodore had held before his election as governor.

In 1914, however, the young man's impatience got the better of him. Just thirty-two years old, he publicly pondered a race for governor or senator as an anti-Tammany Wilsonite. Once satisfied that TR himself would not run as a third-party candidate for governor ("You know blood is thicker than water," he said, ignoring his own efforts in 1912), Franklin flirted with such a nomination himself. Failing to stir interest in that effort, he instead announced his availability for the U.S. Senate, in New York's first direct election for that office. But now it was Murphy who stepped carefully, putting forward James W. Gerard, Wilson's own ambassador to Germany, for the office. The president and his circle stayed neutral in the contest, and Roosevelt, despite flailing away publicly at Murphy, lost the primary to Gerard by nearly 3 to 1.

It was FDR's first electoral defeat. He and Murphy had each drawn blood from the other. In the years surrounding the Great War, they learned to coexist.

At the 1920 Democratic National Convention, however, Roosevelt and Murphy went one more round. On the convention's opening day, Homer Cummings delivered a rousing tribute to the ailing Wilson, touching off a huge demonstration. But Murphy's New York delegation declined to join in.

Shouts of "Get up, New York!" began coming from all over the hall. In accordance with instructions from Murphy, Jeremiah T. Mahoney, a man of bulky build, was firm in his seat gripping the New York standard. . . . The convention saw Roosevelt run over to Mahoney and grab the standard with a vigor which dragged Mahoney off his seat into the aisle. There was a minute or two of scuffling, in which friends came to the aid of each. Then, in Roosevelt's hands the standard joined the parade, with some thirty delegates from New York behind it.

By week's end Franklin Roosevelt, now thirty-eight years old, was the Democratic party's nominee for vice president of the United States. His selection had been ratified by presidential nominee James Cox, governor of Ohio, even after Cox had consulted with Murphy. It was not that Murphy had become a Roosevelt fan, but the boss felt that Roosevelt's presence on the ticket might help the troubled bid of Al Smith for reelection as governor. Once again Roosevelt and Tammany, while adversaries, had found a way for both to come out ahead.

When Murphy died suddenly in 1924, Roosevelt seemed to express genuine loss: "The New York City Democratic organization has lost probably the strongest and wisest leader it has had in generations. He was essentially a man of his word and loyal to his friends. He was a genius who kept harmony, and at the same time recognized that the world moved on."

And Roosevelt's accommodations with the machine Murphy left behind continued. He was no friend of Tammany Hall, but he took pains not to be an enemy either. In 1928, Roosevelt was elected to succeed Smith as governor. When Tammany built a new headquarters at Union Square, Governor Roosevelt spent part of his Fourth of July 1929 giving a rousing anti–big business speech at the dedication ceremonies. Four days later, as if that had not been enough, he mailed a personal check contributing to the building fund.

☐   Roosevelt's respect for Tammany extended to a respect for the tradition informing the selection of state judges from Manhattan. That tradition held that such posts were controlled by Tammany.

One such vacancy, on the state Supreme Court, opened up in January 1930 when Joseph Proskauer announced that he would be leaving the court for the even more lucrative world of high-end private practice. Proskauer had been appointed to the court by Smith in 1922 and elected to a full term in 1924. When he resigned on March 11, 1930, the search for his successor moved into high gear.

While justices of the Supreme Court were elected to office, and in fact to fourteen-year terms, the power to fill vacancies on an interim basis, that is, until the next election, was appointive, and lay with the governor. But the appointment process was well understood to be just as political as the elective one. As the *New York Times* observed, "No one doubts, therefore, that the appointment will go to a party man. Probably it will go to an organization man. This means that it must have the approval of Tammany."

But matters were not nearly as simple as seen from Governor Roosevelt's perspective. On the Proskauer vacancy, FDR was being pulled in at least three directions. First, the Good Government forces, led in this case by the Association of the Bar of the City of New York, sought a candidate whose professional qualifications they had certified. The Bar Association's judiciary committee included 1924 Democratic presidential nominee John W. Davis. It also included Senator Robert Wagner. Second, Tammany had its own favorites. And third, Al Smith and his followers, having only recently lost control of the machine with the election of Walker's ally, John Curry, as its new boss, had their own preferences. The choice seemed almost certain to set back FDR with important elements of his own party, and possibly with reformers in general.

Early in March the governor received the Bar Association's list. Its first choice was City Court Justice Bernard Shientag;

Shientag also had the active support of Al Smith, with whom he was close both personally and politically. But Davis and his colleagues were also prepared to endorse the selection of lawyers Isidor Kresel and Solomon Strook; they advanced as well the name of Ben Schreiber, who had managed political campaigns for both Mayor Walker and Senator Wagner. For a show of bipartisanship, the Bar committee also sent Roosevelt the names of five Republicans, but everyone involved knew that Roosevelt would nominate a Democrat.

It was not a coincidence that all of the Democrats endorsed by the Bar group were, like Proskauer, Jews. Even the Good Government types thought they understood the imperatives of ethnic politics in New York.

On this point Tammany did not disagree. On March 20 the Democratic county committee put forward seven names for the vacancy. Their preferred choice, they made clear, was Maurice Deiches, a former law partner of Ed Flynn, now FDR's secretary of state. Deiches too was Jewish. Most of all, however, he was not Smith's choice but Curry's, another pawn in the battle between the two men. A third faction, led by Mayor Walker and Lieutenant Governor Herbert Lehman, favored yet another Jewish candidate, Jonah Goldstein.

Franklin Roosevelt was in a bind: he was being asked to choose sides in a factional fight within the Jewish community when he needed support from all parts of this key Democratic constituency, and also to pick between Smith and Curry—two internecine brawls within subcultures to which he did not belong. The imperative for a third path, a compromise choice, must have seemed clear to him.

By Sunday, April 6, the legislature's adjournment was approaching, creating a deadline to fill the vacancy, as the

87

governor's choice would require legislative confirmation. On that day Senator Wagner came calling at the executive mansion in Albany and offered the compromise Roosevelt needed. The name he suggested was not even on the original list that his own Bar Association committee had sent to the governor a month earlier, and it was not a name Roosevelt knew well.

Two days after Wagner's Sunday visit, Joseph Crater, no one's first choice, but a Protestant, a loyal Tammany man, and—most important—someone for whom Bob Wagner could vouch, was nominated by Governor Roosevelt to be a justice of the New York State Supreme Court. Crater's name had apparently been included on a larger, supplemental list provided by the Bar Association, and this was important to FDR. (Years later, speaking more generally of Tammany-inspired judicial selections, Roosevelt told Robert Jackson, then his U.S. attorney general, that any Tammany designee for the federal bench "must have the approval of the Bar Association. You know, when I was Governor, I found that was a great protection.")

☐   Who was this man Crater?

The Crater family came from Germany in the eighteenth century and settled in Hunterdon County, New Jersey. Soon they made their way to Easton, Pennsylvania, a town on the Delaware River, situated roughly midway north and south on the state's eastern border. Joe's grandfather, J. F. Crater, founded a successful produce business in Easton, including many acres of orchards, which he passed along to his son Frank, Joe's father. The family was quite comfortable and lived in a large, three-story brick house at Fifth and Ferry streets.

Joe was born at home on January 5, 1889, the first of four children (three boys and a girl) of Frank and his wife Lelia. Joe was too old for mandatory service in the Great War (he was twenty-eight when the United States entered the war in 1917), but his brother Douglas enlisted in the Canadian air force, suffered from shell shock, and died soon after the war ended. His sister, Margaret, moved away when she married, and his brother Montague eventually left for the West.

Joe went to Easton High School, where he was president of his sophomore and junior classes and a member of the Mandolin Club his junior and senior years. His senior class yearbook indicated that he was apparently already self-conscious about his long, thin neck, noting "his abundant supply of gaudy neckwear." The yearbook also observed that "Joe entered High School with the idea of studying for the ministry, but this is only a glimmer of the past. 'Woman' has become his permanent study. He claims to have passed the infants and is now studying the 'Elders' of that sex."

Crater graduated from Easton in 1906 and moved on locally to Lafayette College. His college transcripts show that he placed solidly within the top quarter of his sophomore class but slipped to the middle of the pack in his junior and senior years. He exhibited strength as a student of French and took Latin all four years, the last two of these as an elective; his weakest subject was physics. During his senior year he was one of five students "debarred" in political economy, or delayed in taking his exam because of three unexcused absences.

Crater was a member of the Sigma Chi fraternity. As a member of the Mandolin Club, he joined in concerts throughout Pennsylvania and into New Jersey, and rose from second mandolin in his sophomore and junior years to first mandolin in his senior year. He also showed some interest in politics as a member of the Republican Club during his sophomore year (the last year of TR's presidency), but he switched to the Democratic Club when William Howard Taft became president during his junior year; in his senior year he joined neither party's club. His college senior yearbook made more references to his neckwear and noted cryptically that "He has written an authoritative work on 'Marriage and Neck Ties.' They who know say it's 'good.' "

Crater graduated *cum laude* from Lafayette in 1910 and entered Columbia Law School in New York, from which he graduated in 1913. He had met his future wife in 1912, and they married in 1917.

Crater worked as a law clerk after his graduation from Columbia, and from 1917 onward he also taught law at the City College of New York, Fordham, and New York University. He was active in professional societies as well, serving three years as secretary of the Appellate Division's Special Calendar Committee. This committee, dealing with congestion in the courts, included among its members U.S. Chief Justice Charles Evans Hughes and former Judge Samuel Seabury. Crater also became active in Democratic politics and gave up his post at Fordham in 1919 to allow more time for his activities as a member of the Cayuga Club. Later he also stopped teaching at City College, although he was still instructing NYU night students in the law of torts at the time of his judicial appointment. He became a member of Tammany's law committee.

With greater involvement in politics seemed to come greater prosperity. In 1919, Crater purchased the cabin in Belgrade Lakes, Maine for his wife. He went to work as law secretary for then Justice Wagner in 1920 and stayed in that post almost six years. After he entered private practice, much of it as an appellate advocate on behalf of Wagner's new law firm, the Craters' lives began to change even more dramatically. They bought their Fifth Avenue cooperative apartment in 1927 and moved there after spending three weeks in a Biltmore Hotel suite adjoining that of former Governor Al Smith. They soon hired a cook, the maid Amedia Christian, and the chauffeur Fred Kahler. They bought a grand piano, and Crater paid off his parents' $5,000 mortgage. After less than four years in practice on his own, Crater found himself nominated for the highest judicial post in New York County.

☐ While Crater's selection was a surprise to nearly everyone, he was confirmed by the State Senate within two days and sworn into office just a week after that. Grand Sachem Curry was among those present when Crater took his oath of office.

Roosevelt, while not offending Tammany, had also managed to win plaudits for his independence of the machine. The *New York Law Journal*, in a news article on Crater's nomination, observed that he "has a recognized standing at the Bar as a lawyer of capacity and distinct ability." In an editorial two days later, the *Law Journal* added that FDR "has acted wisely and with sound judgment" in the appointment. Crater's ascension to the bench "undoubtedly marks the commencement of a long and valuable judicial career, begun under happy and comforting auspices."

The *Times* similarly concluded that "No estimate of what [Roosevelt] has done would be fair without considering what he has resisted." Calling the selection "highly gratifying to [the Governor's] friends," the *Times* described Crater as "a lawyer who, in the judgment of members of his profession, is well qualified to be on the bench of the Supreme Court." No basis was cited for this conclusion. It was the last comment the *Times* would make about Crater until his disappearance.

Chapter Five

CRATER
AT THE
VANISHING POINT

☐ Joseph Crater may have gone missing on the evening of Wednesday, August 6, but it was some time before he was missed.

The Craters' maid, Amedia Christian, returned to the 40 Fifth Avenue apartment on the morning of Thursday, August 7, just as the judge had asked her to on Monday. She noted that the bed had been slept in, and presumed that the judge had been there the preceding night. The suit he had worn on Wednesday morning was among clothes he had left for her to give to a local cleaner, and she did so; the suit was cleaned and pressed, and returned the same afternoon.

At Judge Crater's chambers, they expected that he was returning to Maine.

In Maine, Stella Crater had been told by her husband that he would probably be home Wednesday, but certainly no later than Saturday. As there was no telephone in their home, she did not expect further word until he actually arrived. She became a bit anxious Wednesday, but did not go to meet the daily train from New York until Thursday. When the judge was not aboard, she and local friends concluded that he would return the following day, or the day after that.

Saturday, August 9, was Stella's birthday, and a Belgrade Lakes storekeeper delivered a red canoe that Joe had purchased for her as a gift. Friends came to a birthday party for her that evening, working to cheer her up. Still, she later wrote, "I must admit I was not overly concerned at this time. Annoyed is a more apt description." While she did not say so, it was almost certainly not the first time that her husband had kept her waiting and in ignorance of his plans.

By Monday, August 11, Crater was well overdue, and Stella was growing much more concerned. She went to the home of friends and used their telephone to call New York. The person to whom she reached out was Simon Rifkind, Crater's successor as Robert Wagner's law secretary. Some years later, Mrs. Crater testified under oath that Rifkind "reassured me that he had seen him around, he couldn't say just when, that day or the day before, but he asked me if I would like to have him look for him or check to see if he was in town. I told him I would." In fact, Rifkind had not seen Crater for five days.

The work week passed, and Rifkind, despite his assurances to a worried wife, did not contact her. He and his part-

Joseph Force Crater, in a photo taken at around the time of his appointment to the New York State Supreme Court. Self-conscious about his unusually thin neck, he continued to wear stiff collars even as they went out of style. (*Library of Congress*)

Stella Mance Wheeler Crater, much later in life, with the note Joe left behind. (© *The New York Times*)

The sachems of Tammany Hall, circa 1870. The fat man seated second
to the right of table at center is Boss William Marcy Tweed. Tweed and
his small band of cronies stole the modern equivalent of $1.1 billion over
the course of twelve years. (*National Archives*)

The new headquarters of Tammany Hall (the "Wigwam") at Union Square.
Governor Franklin D. Roosevelt gave the dedication speech, July 4, 1929,
and sent a personal check for the building fund. (© *The New York Times*)

The leaders of Tammany Hall at the dedication of the new Wigwam.
Left to right, former surrogate James Foley, Mayor Jimmy Walker, Grand
Sachem John Voorhis, former governor Al Smith, Tammany leader John
Curry. (© *Bettmann/CORBIS*)

Governor Al Smith and Justice Robert Wagner (swinging) on the links,
1926. At Charles Murphy's command they had become their party's
leaders in the legislature at the ages of thirty-seven and thirty-three,
respectively. (© *Bettmann/CORBIS*)

Justice Robert Wagner administers the oath of office as mayor to Jimmy Walker, January 1925. Anti-German feeling kept Wagner from the mayoralty in 1917; his Protestantism prevented his leading Tammany in the 1920s. (© *The New York Times*)

Jimmy Walker aboard ship, 1930. In his first two years in office he spent 143 days on vacation. (© *Bettmann/CORBIS*)

Representative
Fiorello La Guardia,
in a House office
building, mocks
Prohibition by mixing
two legal beverages to
create an illegal one,
1926. Challenged to
repeat the stunt
without the cloak
of congressional
immunity, he
promptly did so at a
drug store in Harlem.
(© *Bettmann/CORBIS*)

La Guardia, Republican
candidate for mayor, on
Election Day 1929, just
before his overwhelming
defeat by Walker. In 1930 he
declared, "I can say to the
people who voted against me
last year, 'I told you so.'"
(© *The New York Times*)

Tammany leader Charles Murphy and Assistant Secretary of the Navy Franklin Roosevelt, 1917. At Murphy's death in 1924, Roosevelt called him "a genius who kept harmony." (© *Bettmann/CORBIS*)

The incoming and outgoing governors of New York, 1928–1929: Franklin Roosevelt and Al Smith. It was a speech delivered by Roosevelt (though written by Justice Joseph Proskauer) that dubbed Smith the "Happy Warrior." (*Brown Brothers*)

Jimmy Walker arrives to testify, 1932. "Little Boy Blue is about to blow his horn—or his top." (*AP/Wide World*)

Samuel Seabury examines Walker. "There are three things a man must do alone: Be born, die, and testify." (© *The New York Times*)

Walker emerges after testifying. He "left the witness stand trailing clouds not of glory but of mystery." (© *The New York Times*)

Fiorello La Guardia is sworn in as mayor of the City of New York by
Justice Philip McCook, New Year's Eve, 1933–1934. Samuel Seabury,
in whose home the ceremony took place, stands between them.
(© *Bettmann/CORBIS*)

ner, Francis Quillinan, who was also Al Smith's son-in-law, may have made telephone inquiries to the race tracks at Saratoga, to Toronto, where the show *Artists and Models* was then playing, and to Montreal, but there is no indication that they located Crater.

By Friday, August 15, Stella Crater moved to take matters more directly into her own hands. She dispatched Fred Kahler, the Craters' chauffeur, who had remained behind in Maine when the judge had taken the train back to New York, to the family's Fifth Avenue apartment. Kahler arrived Friday night or Saturday and found a substantial quantity of unopened mail.

Perhaps Kahler contacted Rifkind—that would certainly have made sense. In any event, Rifkind apparently finally sent Mrs. Crater a telegram, likely on Saturday the 16th. The next day she acknowledged it with a letter of her own. "Dear Mr. Rifkind," she wrote,

> Many thanks for your wire. As I had not heard from Joe since Aug. 3, was beginning to wonder if he was still alive. Sorry to trouble you, and again many thanks.
>
> Sincerely, Mrs. Crater
>
> P.S. If you happen to see him, I do need some money.

Rifkind clearly had told her some sort of reassuring lie.

A couple of days later, Kahler took a similar line with his employer, relying perhaps on Rifkind as well as others. In a note sent to her in Maine, he wrote,

> Dear Mrs. Crater:
>
> It looks as if everything is all right. The apartment is OK. I haven't seen Mr. Crater but everybody says he has been around and is all right.

95

On August 22, Kahler returned to Maine, but he also brought Stella a disquieting report. Crater's associates, he said, had discouraged him from looking too actively—too visibly—for the judge. News of such an inquiry, they warned, could damage his chances for election to a full fourteen-year term on the Supreme Court in the fall. No such news had appeared anywhere, and they sought to keep it that way. Fred Johnson, Crater's law secretary, was one of those who delivered this message to Kahler. Johnson later testified that he had also falsely told Kahler that he had seen Crater, out of a desire to protect their mutual employer.

Crater was due to preside at a Supreme Court term beginning Monday, August 25. By this time Stella, still in Maine, was, by her own later account, sleep deprived, barely eating, nearly incoherent. When Crater failed to appear in court, the chief judge, Louis Valente, called Stella at a public telephone in Belgrade Lakes, to which neighbors summoned her. It is possible that Valente also spoke during this call with Kahler, whom Valente had previously employed.

In any event, it was only at this point—or, at the latest, during another call to Mrs. Crater from Simon Rifkind two days later—that all concerned seem to have become convinced that Joseph Crater was truly missing. Still, they told almost no one.

Instead, the instinct to try to resolve the matter privately, presumably to avoid embarrassment, political or otherwise, continued to prevail. But they did begin to take action. Leo Lowenthal, Senator Wagner's bodyguard and a former New York City Police Department detective, began a search for Crater on the day after Valente's call. Lowenthal later said he did so "for personal reasons"; it seems very likely that he was working on behalf of Valente, Rifkind, or both.

Lowenthal interviewed Crater's confidential assistant, Joseph Mara, as one of his first orders of business, and later said that he had quickly learned of the judge's document destruction and removal on August 6. Lowenthal did not consider this a reason to alert the police. Mara had been regularly calling at 40 Fifth Avenue for the Craters' mail since Kahler's visit two weeks earlier. On August 28, Mara and another man, probably Lowenthal, sought to enter the apartment itself but were refused the key by the building's superintendent.

☐ In the midst of this mild search, on August 15, despite what seemed to many the clear evidence that a bribe had been offered and accepted, a grand jury impaneled by the district attorney of New York County declined to return any indictments in the judgeship-selling case of Magistrate Ewald and District Leader Healy. By August 26 the Ewald–Healy investigation had become sufficiently embarrassing that the Appellate Division of the Supreme Court, the tribunal charged with managing the bar and the lower courts, moved to appoint a special investigator of the city's Magistrates' Courts. Their choice, the secret recommendation of Governor Roosevelt, was Samuel Seabury, a living symbol of rectitude itself.

Seabury was not the usual sort of New York prosecutor. He learned of his appointment only the following day, for instance, because he was on a summer holiday in London. At the moment of his notification, he later let it be known, he had just found in an antiquarian bookshop a long-sought copy of a 1630 first edition of *The Just Lawyer*.

Samuel Seabury, however, did not invent such a self-righteous persona. He inherited it.

In a city in which the great waves of immigration had begun just thirty or so years before his birth, Seabury was a ninth-generation American, the fifth of the nine to bear the name Samuel. The first American Samuel Seabury, literally a Puritan, had arrived in 1639, but our Samuel was also descended directly from John Alden—who had been too shy to speak for himself—and the lovely, and legendary, Priscilla Mullens. The third Samuel had become the first Episcopal bishop in America and had seen it his duty to remain loyal to the Crown even in the face of the American Revolution. The family crest bore a motto in Latin, *Supera Alta Tenere*, Hold to the Most High.

In this context Samuel Seabury himself, born in the rectory of the Church of the Annunciation to an unbroken line of five generations of clerics, was something of a rebel. He was attracted to reform politics at a young age and denounced the practice of selling judgeships as early as 1899, when he said publicly that "it is a disgrace for Supreme Court justices to pay from $10,000 to $20,000 to political organizations for their places." Seabury supported the successful Fusion mayoral candidacy of William Strong and campaigned for a seat as an alderman at the age of twenty-four. But he gave up that campaign to devote his full energies to the "single tax" utopian crusade of Henry George, author of *Progress and Poverty*, for the mayoralty.

George died before the election, and his son, running in his place, was defeated, but Seabury remained involved, and in 1901, at age twenty-eight, was elected as New York's youngest City Court judge. He served almost fifteen years as a judge, although he simultaneously remained active in Democratic and Fusion politics, supporting first William Jennings Bryan and then Woodrow Wilson at the national level, and mayors Seth Low and John Purroy Mitchel in New York. In 1905 he declined the mayoral nomination of William Randolph Hearst's Municipal Ownership League and instead helped engineer Hearst's own nomination for mayor. In 1906 he supported Hearst for governor.

In the same year Seabury was elected to the State Supreme Court, again, at thirty-three, the youngest to hold the office. By 1909 he had split with Hearst, sensing that the publisher's ambitions were beginning to undermine the policies he ostensibly favored—not to mention Seabury's own advancement within the Democratic party. In 1914, running as a candidate of both the Democrats and Theodore Roosevelt's "Bull Moose" Progressives, Seabury was elected to a term on the state's highest court, the Court of Appeals.

Now the prospect of even greater glory drew him more directly into partisan politics, and the experience proved an unhappy one. Seabury won a primary in 1916 as the Democratic nominee for governor of New York, securing the right to oppose incumbent Governor Charles Whitman in the general election. But Tammany, which Seabury and his Fusion allies had always opposed, withheld its active support. Hearst, then still a power in New York politics, also refused to back Seabury.

The Judge (as he ever after preferred to be known) believed that he held a trump card, however—TR's Progressives. It was Roosevelt, in fact, who had persuaded Seabury to resign from the court to seek the gubernatorial nomination. "You may assuredly count" on the Progressives, TR said. "I never will give my support to Whitman." But the former president, having entered the national fray as the Bull Moose champion and dragged down the Republican party and his chosen successor William Howard Taft to a humiliating third-place finish in the 1912 presidential election, was now seeking his way back inside the GOP tent in anticipation of another run in 1920. Seabury became an obstacle to that, and TR betrayed him. The Progressive nod went to Whitman.

Seabury lost the 1916 election. Not long afterward he confronted Roosevelt at his home in Oyster Bay. "Mr. President," he snarled, "you are a blatherskite!" There is no record of Roosevelt's reaction.

Disillusioned, Seabury retired to private life but soon made the most of it. His lucrative law practice enabled him to own both a large townhouse on East Sixty-third Street in Manhattan and a six-hundred-acre farm in East Hampton. At the latter he built a two-story library with space for ten thousand books, many of them rare. His collection included first editions of volumes by Hobbes, Locke, Mill, and Blackstone— and Machiavelli.

Seabury may have been a lifelong reformer, but he was certainly no man of the people, and now he did not need to pretend otherwise. "His pince-nez glasses, center-parted white hair, and starched look gave him an aloof, superior air," Herbert Mitgang has written. Another author noted that "He was never heard to use slang or indulge in a wisecrack, and his presence was such that he could invest the blowing of his nose with theological overtones." His associates joked that anyone who called him "Sam" would be struck by lightning.

In 1907 a Seabury judicial decision had given rise to an investigation of New York County District Attorney William Travers Jerome. Confronting his accuser at the ensuing hearing, Jerome asked Seabury,

> "Mr. Justice, will you be good enough to express your honest opinion of me?"
> "Do you want my honest opinion?"
> "I do."
> "I find it impossible to raise you to the level of my contempt."

Nor did he mellow with age. At one point in an investigative hearing more than twenty years later, a state senator turned to Seabury and remarked, apropos of nothing in particular, that he had heard that the Judge had garnered a one-million-dollar fee from an accounting of the estate of the legendary robber baron Jay Gould. "Yes," Seabury said, he had earned such a fee "over a ten-year period." "But I never heard of anyone receiving such an amount. *I* never got such a fee," the senator noted. "Senator," Samuel Seabury replied, "the reason is obvious—you were never worth that much to anybody."

☐ On the same day Detective Lowenthal and Crater assistant Joseph Mara were refused access to the Craters' apartment, Stella Crater decided she could take the waiting no more. She had Fred Kahler drive her back to New York. They arrived in the city in the early hours of Friday, August 29. As she later wrote, ". . . as soon as we reached the apartment, I dashed upstairs and started telephoning everyone of whom I could think."

Unlike many of Stella's recollections, this one was strictly accurate. At 2:45 A.M. she called Crater's Tammany district leader, Martin Healy, and spoke with him for seven minutes. Healy described her as "hysterical." That night or the next morning she also called Simon Rifkind and Mayor Walker. There is no indication that the mayor took any action after this call. At 12:15 P.M. on the 29th she called the Healy home again and spoke for six minutes, this time with Martin Healy's mother. Healy recalled that he had telephoned Stella from someplace else Friday morning, and had urged her to speak with Fred Johnson. Lowenthal, soon after, recalled that he had been present in the Crater apartment for at least some of these calls—although presumably not the one at just before three o'clock in the morning. Lowenthal said, "I'm as positive as I'm standing here that she wasn't faking. She was hysterical and it wasn't any pose."

Lowenthal also helped Stella search the apartment. They found, according to her, that only one of her husband's suits was missing—the brown pinstripe in which he'd been seen at Billy Haas's restaurant more than three weeks earlier, notable because its matching vest was still hanging in the closet. What puzzled her more than what was missing was what was *not*: "his cherished monogrammed pocket watch, pen and card case, all of which he ordinarily carried."

Having learned little from the search, but still apparently very concerned that the matter was almost out of hand, Lowenthal prevailed on Stella to return to Maine on Saturday, August 30. She should, he said, await Senator Wagner's return from Europe, which was expected within a few days. "I don't think anything should be done until he gets here."

As we shall see, Stella Crater may well have made a re-markable discovery during the apartment search. But if she did so, she kept it to herself.

Someone, however, was not so discreet. Over the next day or two, news of Judge Crater's disappearance was related to George Hall, a reporter for the *New York World*. Hall's story was not published until Wednesday, September 3, after the Labor Day holiday, but it had clearly been in the works for some time; it ran thirty-three column inches, and was quite detailed. Many of the details were accurately reported; some were not.

The *World* headline was "Justice J. F. Crater/Missing From His/Home Since Aug. 6." The lead paragraph of the story identified Crater as a "former law associate" of Wagner's. The story accurately noted that Crater had last been seen August 6, that he had bought a ticket for a Broadway show that night from an agency, and that he had cashed large checks earlier that day. It correctly noted his six years' work for Wagner and explained that Crater was president of Martin Healy's Cayuga Democratic Club, although "The presidency of a Tammany club is virtually perfunctory, the leader always being the actual and active head of the organization."

But the article inaccurately stated that his chauffeur and law secretary (Kahler and Johnson, though neither was named in the article) had missed the judge on the morning of August 7, and had both notified his wife and checked local hospitals. And it stated that the Craters lived at 303 West 122nd Street, which was the address listed in the telephone directory— and on the voting rolls.

(This last error was corrected the following day by the *Herald Tribune*, which said Crater used the 122nd Street address "as a voting residence so that he might comply with the law and not be forced to break political ties when he moved to a more prosperous neighborhood." In other words, Crater broke the law on the simple matter of where he lived. But he was not alone in doing so. The *New York Sun* soon referred to the 122nd Street building as a "political nest.")

With the publication of the story in the *World* on September 3, as these follow-ups on such a minor side issue as Crater's legal address make clear, a frenzy of reporting immediately began. Articles appeared in late editions of the September 3 *Herald Tribune* and *Daily News*; the afternoon *Sun* carried a full story on its front page. That afternoon, Hearst's *American* sent a telegram to Governor Roosevelt asking "at whose instance Crater was appointed to the bench and who his sponsors were." The next morning the *New York Times* joined the fray with a front-page account. As with the article in the *World*, and nearly all that followed, the *Times* mixed speculation and reporting, fact and fiction.

☐ Simon Rifkind had known something was amiss with Joseph Crater since August 11. But only on September 3, as the first reports of Crater's disappearance were published, did Rifkind seek to involve the New York Police Department. He did so by contacting Police Commissioner Edward Mulrooney and requesting the department's help in locating Crater. Fifty years later Rifkind told the *New Yorker* that he had filed the missing person's report only because Fred Johnson, Crater's law secretary, had delayed in doing so. But Rifkind neglected to tell the *New Yorker*'s John Brooks that he had known of Crater's disappearance well before Johnson did.

At almost the same moment Rifkind opened the missing person's case, however, he sought effectively to close it—and to contain the political damage. Rifkind told the *New York Times* on September 3 that he believed that Crater had been murdered; he repeated that belief—based on what, he said not—to the *New York Sun* the next day. Even more important, Rifkind asserted that Crater's disappearance (and murder, if that it had been) was unrelated to the Ewald–Healy investigation.

On the question of the Ewald connection, the newspapers were not so sure. They quickly noted that Crater had presided at the ceremony when, on May 12, 1927, Ewald had been sworn in as a magistrate. And they noted that Crater had also acted as toastmaster when the event was soon celebrated at a dinner at the Concourse Plaza Hotel in the Bronx. The *Sun's* headline called Crater "Ewald's friend."

In the interviews he gave, Rifkind made no mention of the call he had received from Stella Crater in Maine on August 11, nor of the wire he sent her after that, nor of her call to him from the New York apartment later in the month. Given the questions he was asked, there can be no doubt that Rifkind's omissions were intentional. And the picture Rifkind painted in public of Crater was disingenuous in the extreme. In words that may have accurately descibed himself, but certainly fell wide of the mark with respect to Joe Crater, Rifkind told the *Sun* that the jurist "avoided public affairs or receptions, and denied himself creature comforts. He was extremely careful of his conduct in all because he wanted no discredit to attach itself to him." Meanwhile, on September 4, Rifkind moved to shore up Stella Crater's finances by retrieving the judge's paychecks and depositing them to the

Craters' joint account; he also made the first of two loans to Stella, for $200. (Another loan of $1,000 followed less than two weeks later.)

More troubling to Rifkind, no doubt, were the articles linking Judge Crater to Senator Wagner. The initial *World* story went the furthest, calling Wagner "perhaps [Crater's] closest friend." On September 4, the second day of the public phase of the Crater mystery, Wagner's ship, the North German Lloyd liner *Bremen*, was due to dock in New York as he returned from his summer vacation in Europe.

Having learned of the stories about Crater's disappearance by radiograms received aboard ship, and unwilling to wait even until he docked, Wagner sent a radiogram to the *World* taking exception to their characterization of his relationship with Crater. He wrote of his law office colleague, his law secretary of six years, a man who had seen him off on this very same cruise five weeks earlier: "I have absolutely no knowledge or information about his personal or business affairs." The senator added that he had seen Crater only two or three times since May, and that the two men had not been in contact since Wagner sailed for Europe.

In New York the next day, Crater was the main subject that reporters meeting the *Bremen* wanted to talk about with Wagner. Now the senator went even further, went over the line into clear deceit, saying that he and Crater "were never more than mere acquaintances." Wagner asserted that he had opposed Roosevelt's nomination of Crater for the Supreme Court, having favored Shientag, the choice of Smith and the Bar Association. He did allow that he had told FDR that Crater "was a very competent man," but ostensibly not more than that. The assembled press seems to have swallowed whole this rewriting of very recent history. The *New York Times* deadpanned, "It had generally been believed until yesterday, when he denied it, that Senator Wagner's intervention had obtained the office for Justice Crater."

That evening, back in the privacy of his city apartment with just a few close aides and family, including Rifkind and a Wagner niece, Wagner was seen to be "boiling mad" and took to "whacking a golf ball about the living room."

Meanwhile, theories about what had happened to Crater diverged. Crater's colleagues in the courts echoed Rifkind's line that they believed he had been killed—certainly a curious approach for friends in the first days of an official investigation. On the other hand, the police commissioner offered the view that the judge had disappeared intentionally, noting his destruction of documents and the monogrammed items he had left behind.

By Friday, September 5, Judge Crater was New York's latest obsession. The front page of Thursday's *World* had carried the headline "Crater Mystery Deepens;/No Clue to Whereabouts/Police Making No Search." A frantic police search ensued, and suddenly Crater, simply on the basis of a few photographs published in the newspapers, was being "sighted" everywhere, from Rouse's Point, New York, to Toronto and Montreal. New York Police Department detectives were dispatched to check each sighting, only to find them groundless. Newspaper reporters followed them—and fanned out elsewhere, interviewing the judge's father in Orlando, Florida, for instance, on Sunday, September 7.

Meanwhile, Stella Crater remained in Maine, in seclusion. On Saturday, September 6, she formally sought to make a missing person's report to the NYPD. The next day she was visited at her home in Belgrade Lakes by Detective Edward Fitzgerald and gave him a brief, informal interview.

The Police Department followed the next day, Monday, with a formal circular. Headlined "Missing Since August 6, 1930," it contained a formal photographic portrait of Crater above the caption, "Honorable Joseph Force Crater, Justice of the Supreme Court, State of New York." It described Crater as follows:

> Born in the United States—Age, 41 years; height, 6 feet; weight, 185 pounds; mixed grey hair, originally dark brown, thin at top, parted in middle "slicked" down; complexion, medium dark, considerably tanned; brown eyes; false teeth, upper and lower jaw, good physical and mental condition at time of disappearance. Tip of right index finger somewhat mutilated; due to having been recently crushed. Wore brown sack coat and trousers, narrow green stripe, no vest; either a Panama or soft brown hat worn at rakish angle, size 6 5/8, unusual size for his height and weight. Clothes made by Vroom. Affected colored shirts, size 14 collar, probably bow tie. Wore tortoise-shell glasses for reading. Yellow gold Masonic ring, somewhat worn; may be wearing a yellow gold, square-shaped wrist watch with yellow strap.

Curiously, especially for such a fulsome description, the Sigma Chi fraternity tattoo on one of Crater's arms was omitted.

On the same day, NYPD Detective Hugh Sheridan and a colleague made a second search of the Craters' Fifth Avenue apartment; the first search had been made by Detective Fitzgerald four days earlier. How thoroughly Sheridan searched the Craters' bedroom would later become a key issue in the case.

As the missing person's circular began to make its way around the country, Al Smith the next day laid the cornerstone for the rising Empire State Building. The former governor took the occasion to sum up the history of the site: "Eighty years ago, a very short time when one stops to think, this land was part of a farm. More recently it was the site of one of the great hotels of the world [the Waldorf-Astoria], and soon it will be the location of the tallest structure ever built by man." But just as Smith's dream was rising, Joseph Crater's reputation was about to come crashing to earth.

Elaine Dawn, the aspiring actress with whom Crater had spent the evening of August 4 at Club Abbey, had gone from her room at the Plymouth Hotel to one at Polyclinic Hospital on August 17. She was reportedly suffering from "rheumatism" or "rheumatic knee," and was forced to leave the tour of her show, *Artists and Models*, before it moved from New York to Toronto. Rumors of a connection between Crater and Dawn must have been swirling among reporters—the presence of *Artists and Models* in Toronto was probably responsible for the tip placing Crater in that city—but not a word had appeared publicly.

Now Miss Dawn, described as a small blonde, an "attractive brown-eyed young woman with a Southern accent," permitted reporters to come into her hospital room. There she gave interviews about her relationship to the judge. She told the *Sun* that she had met Crater over the summer and had been introduced to him by William Klein, the Shubert organization attorney. Of Crater, Miss Dawn (another showgirl offered the information that her real name was Orlay), said, "He knew several girls in the 'Artists and Models' troupe when I was in it, and they all liked him."

With that the scandal gathered momentum, offering not only political intrigue but sex.

The day after the interviews with Dawn were published, the *New York Daily News* linked Crater as well to Sally Lou Ritz, the woman with whom he and William Klein had dined on the night of August 6, and with Alice Woods, a fellow cast member of Dawn's in *Artists and Models*. Woods and Crater, it soon developed, had also met earlier in the summer and had spent some time together in June. On June 27, Crater had sent a telegram to Alice Woods at her home on South Broadway in Yonkers: "Away for a few weeks. Best regards and luck—Joe." Woods now said that she had not seen Crater since then. "We were only friends," she insisted. "And not friends in the Broadway sense, either." Further reports added another *Artists and Models* cast member to the list of Crater's women friends: Jane Manners. Yet another showgirl, Emmita Casanova, said Crater had been friendly with at least six women in the *Artists and Models* cast. The search for Crater was extended to Chicago, the latest stop on the show's tour.

The following day, Atlantic City, New Jersey, was added to the list of suspect locales as the name of another woman friend of Crater's was published. She was Marie Miller, a nightclub hostess at the Beaux Arts Club there, and she was said to have been in Crater's company during his visit to the ocean resort in the last days of July. Miller told the *New York Times* that she had spent one evening with Crater; the *Sun* said the encounter stretched over three evenings. All accounts agreed that Crater had come to Atlantic City with Joseph Grainsky, a broker with the Arrow Ticket Agency—the agency where he would pick up his ticket for *Dancing Partner* on the evening of August 6—and Grainsky's friend

Harry Charnas of Warner Bros. Pictures. Crater, Miller, and a number of friends saw a preview of *Dancing Partner* during this visit.

But the Crater affair was becoming more than just a risqué sideshow. Walter Lippmann, the editorial-page editor of the *World*, the newspaper that had broken the story of the judge's disappearance, wrote on the same day as the Alice Woods disclosure that "until this mystery is explained, it will continue to add to the deep uneasiness of the public concerning the judiciary." The NYPD looked for Crater wherever anyone claimed to have spotted him—in Lake George and Troy, New York; Atlantic City; and Fairhaven and Whitehall, Vermont—but Lippmann was losing patience with the lack of results from the investigation. "If the police have gone as far as they can go, it is time for some agency to take a hand." The *World* suggested an inquiry led by a grand jury to be convened by the district attorney of New York County.

When the district attorney, Thomas Crain, moved to launch a magistrate's inquiry instead of a grand jury, Lippmann became insistent, charging that Crain had avoided "the obvious method of procedure" and noting that the magistrate would lack the power to go forward. By September 13, as the police search for Crater had widened to include Raquette Lake, Tupper Lake, and St. Hubert's in upstate New York and the Willard Hotel in Washington, D.C. (where Atlantic City hostess Miller was said to have been spotted), Lippmann had written four editorials in as many days. On the fourth day Crain succumbed to the pressure and announced that a grand jury would look into Crater's disappearance. It had been ten days since news of the matter had become public—and thirty-seven days since Joseph Crater had last been seen.

Crain's grand jury in the Crater case began hearing testimony on September 15—the very day the district attorney's fecklessness cost him control over the Ewald–Healy investigation. Responding to public outrage after Crain's grand jury had reported no charges in the Ewald matter, Governor Roosevelt had been compelled to transfer the lead in that investigation to state prosecutors. As Lippmann would soon recognize, seeking to put Crain in control of the Crater inquiry was a case of not being careful about what you wish for.

Samuel Seabury later called Crain "an ineffectual but honest man surrounded by thieves." Crain was well born and well connected. His father had been American consul in Milan, and Crain himself had been a member of Tammany's General Committee at the age of twenty-seven. Three years later, as the new century began, he was named city chamberlain. Crain had served as a justice on the Court of General Sessions, and then on the Supreme Court, where in 1911 he presided over the trial for murder of the owners of the Triangle Waist Company. Crain had been installed in both judicial posts by Tammany, and John Curry had him named district attorney at the age of sixty-nine. Crain immediately promised to resolve within two weeks the year-old case of the murder of gambler and gangster Arnold Rothstein. A year later the promise remained unfulfilled, and Crain was widely ridiculed.

Mostly, according to a contemporary observer, he was miscast:

> Crain's temperament, in so far as he had any temperament at all, was judicial; he had neither the vigor, the youth, nor

the attitude of mind necessary in the District Attorney's office. His only asset as a candidate was his unchallenged respectability; he was a prominent Episcopal churchman, he lived quietly with two maiden sisters in an old New York mansion, and his inherited fortune amounted to two or three million dollars.

Crain was thus probably not the best choice to lead an investigation whose aim was to locate Joseph Crater. But it was becoming increasingly clear that not everyone involved had that aim.

On September 9 the *World* had offered a reward of $2,500 for information establishing the cause of Crater's disappearance—but it had stipulated that the information be provided not to the Police Department but to the newspaper. The next day Mayor Walker moved to up the ante, seeking an additional reward of $5,000 from the Board of Aldermen. But it was five days before the Board acted. Even then, a one-hour delay was occasioned by difficulties in assembling a quorum.

On the same day the Board did vote the reward, the *World* reported that "Detectives believe the missing jurist had an appointment with a young woman that evening." Yet Garret Hiers, an assistant hotel manager who with his wife Clara had become the Craters' best friends as a couple, refused to help the detectives pursue that line of inquiry and rejected all of the mounting evidence of the judge's womanizing, calling him "a family man, a home man."

When Crain's grand jury convened, prominent Tammany figures continued to advance the theory—now under oath— that Crater was dead. Supreme Court justices William Allen and Alfred Frankenthaler testified to that effect. Justice Valente, the presiding justice in Crater's court, shared with reporters after he testified what he had told the grand jurors: "I'm sure he is dead. We traced him to Club Abbey but then we lost his trail. I believe, like many of his friends, that he flashed a large roll of bills and was taken for a ride."

This testimony raised a host of questions: Who was the "we" who had "traced him"? Presumably Leo Lowenthal, but acting on whose behalf? Why did Valente believe that Crater had returned to Club Abbey, which he had definitely visited on August 4, on August 6? What basis was there for the imputation of motive—robbery of Crater's "large roll of bills"? Crain's prosecutors do not appear to have asked any of these questions, nor did the hordes of reporters covering every development in the case.

On September 12, Stella Crater had received a note demanding a $20,000 ransom for her husband. It had been mailed from New York on or about September 4, the day after the story had broken publicly. It was likely the work of a crank, but when Stella's brother-in-law sought to present the note to the grand jury on September 16, Crain's associates declined even to call him in to testify.

But while District Attorney Crain's grand jury may not have been much of an investigative tool, it was inspiring a fair amount of drama.

By September 15, Stella Crater had been interviewed twice by NYPD detectives, but these interviews were informal, and Mrs. Crater was distraught and not entirely coherent. So Crain sought to pin down her account by means of obtaining written answers to twenty-nine questions mailed to

Mrs. Crater in Maine. The answers were provided in conjunction with the second interview.

☐ Stella Mance Wheeler was two and half years younger than Joe Crater. She was born in Pine Bush, New York, the middle child of three girls. Her father Frank ran the village general store, and her parents always intended for their daughters to work. Stella graduated from the local grammar school and then was sent to Miss Conklin's "secretarial school for young ladies" in Middletown, fourteen miles away. She boarded there during the week for two years, accompanied by her older sister Adelaide.

Duly certified by Miss Conklin, the teenaged Wheeler girls were dispatched to a boardinghouse in New York City, where Stella worked at a "wholesale millinery establishment" for six dollars a week and later as a bookkeeper at the Eric Brothers Fifth Avenue department store. While employed at Eric Brothers, as she later recalled, "I met a young man to whom I suddenly found myself married. The marriage lasted a very short time, and we soon separated." Stella's account does not mention the young man's name or anything else about him. After her separation she went to work, again as a bookkeeper, at the Joseph Baer agency, and then moved on to the Henry Haupt advertising firm. At the age of twenty-five, Stella Wheeler had already lived quite a lot for a girl from Pine Bush.

It was at this point, in March 1912, that she met Joe Crater, then a law student at Columbia, at a dance to which she had been taken by another Columbia law student. "And from that day forward I dated no one else and neither did Joe, I am sure, no matter what was to be said and written about him in light of later events."

After Joe Crater graduated from Columbia Law School in 1913, he took a $25-per-week job as a law clerk. Somewhere along the way he helped Stella with the legal aspects of securing a divorce. After he got a raise to $30 per week, and following five years of dating, he and Stella were married on March 16, 1917, at a Methodist parsonage on Manhattan's Upper West Side. Stella did not work again during the thirteen years of their marriage. She also professed to know little or nothing of her husband's work.

☐ Stella's answers to District Attorney Crain's twenty-nine written questions might be most generously described as succinct. Thirteen of her responses were limited to one word. Four others, including questions seeking information on Crater's bank accounts, safe-deposit boxes, and brokers, consisted of "I don't know." She also didn't know, she wrote, whom Crater "would be most likely to communicate with, aside from [herself], if he were in distress or in trouble." And one question, about the judge's "most intimate social friends and their addresses," was left unanswered entirely. Did she have any idea where her husband was? "No." Had he ever before "absented himself" without letting her know where we was? Again, "No." Had she noticed anything strange recently? Had the judge suffered from memory loss? Did he have any enemies? "No," "No," and "No."

Not only did Stella fail to be forthcoming in response to questions from those who were ostensibly seeking to find her husband, she also failed to tell the truth. One of the questions and answers was as follows:

Q: Who was the first person you communicated with when you suspected he had disappeared?
A: I did not suspect any disappearance. My first intimation of same was a telephone call from Mr. Simon Rifkind on Aug. 26 that he had not appeared in court Aug. 25.

Perhaps trying to follow the line Rifkind had taken in his interviews with the newspapers, Mrs. Crater omitted a host of relevant events: her August 11 telephone call from Maine to Rifkind; her August 15 dispatch of her chauffeur to New York; Rifkind's reassuring telegram to her and her grateful reply; the chauffeur's own reassuring note and then his report that he had been asked not to pose too many questions lest he cause the judge political harm; and, finally and curiously, the fact that the first call when Crater failed to appear in court had come not from Rifkind but from Justice Valente.

Stella lied again when she wrote that she had not "received any moneys from anybody since Aug. 5, 1930, which may have come from him indirectly or which were advanced to you on his account." This omitted the judge's paychecks retrieved by Rifkind and deposited in the Craters' joint account, as well as the $200 loan Rifkind had made to her just eleven days earlier.

Even before publicly releasing these written questions and answers, Crain called Stella's responses "very unsatisfactory." Maine was beyond the reach of his subpoena power, he recognized, but he declared, "I am going to have her here and will leave no stone unturned in bringing about her personal appearance before the grand jury."

That got Stella's dander up. Apparently rallying from her despondency, she now told reporters, through a relative, that she considered Crain's grand jury a "burlesque," although she hastened to clarify her remarks the next day: she had meant, the relative now indicated, that the newspapers themselves were making a burlesque of the inquiry.

No matter the clarification, Crain too was now engaged—perhaps enraged as well. On September 22, just five days after releasing the written examination of the wife of the missing man, the district attorney said he believed that Crater might have returned to Maine before he disappeared, and that Crain now considered Crater's wife a possible suspect in his disappearance. He would seek, Crain said, an investigation of the matter by authorities in Maine, including a search of the Crater house in Belgrade Lakes. But a Maine investigator sent to the house was turned away by Stella's brother-in-law, who told the investigator that Mrs. Crater was ill—indeed, that she had not eaten since the last visit from New York detectives, and often wept. As Stella herself later recalled the incident,

> The sky spun and I fell on my knees near a lilac bush and vomited again and again.
> "Oh God," I sobbed aloud in the dusk of the evening, "they think I killed him."
> Then I fell forward on my face in a dead faint and how long I lay there I do not know.

☐ On September 17, just as District Attorney Crain was commenting on Stella Crater's answers to his interrogatories, another arena opened up in the Crater circus, as the *World* received an anonymous letter addressed to its city editor, dated September 17 in Chicago but postmarked from there September 15. The letter appeared to be from a woman who began it by writing that she was "inclined to withhold my name," yet concluded it by signing a name then withheld by the *World* as likely a pseudonym.

The letter writer said that "she" knew "where Justice Crater is—and so do others." Crater was "in the West," the letter continued, and had gone there after "a tremendous domestic quarrel, which almost shook the roofs of their 5th Ave. apartment." (The letter actually said that Crater's departure "preceeded" the quarrel—presumably because the writer knew neither the spelling nor meaning of "preceded.")

The names mentioned as being in the know were a mixed bunch. "Captain Taylor Phillips" was said to be a "former law-partner of Senator Wagner, the two wives being on intimate terms with each other." But Phillips was not a former Wagner partner, and Wagner's wife had died some years earlier. The writer said,

> I understand that a brother of Lieutenant Governor Lehman and a gentleman with the initials L. R. is also involved. Senator Robert F. Wagner could also shed a little light on the subject. I am more than certain that in less than one week millions in the United States will be reliefed [sic] of this latest mystery of the unexpected disappearance of a noted figure in the social, judicial and political life of America.

But one of the unlikely allegations in the letter received immediate confirmation. The writer said that Judge Crater, as his wife allegedly knew, had to take out of the cash from the bank to satisfy the whine of a "scanty" who threatened scandals. . . .

Dr. Samuel Buckler, former Deputy Attorney General of New York State . . . has been hired as attorney by the complainant to institute an action against the Judge. I also have learned that the case was closed in consideration of $5000 paid by Justice Crater to Buckler's client.

"Buckler" was Dr. Samuel Buchler, a man with a remarkable past. As the letter said, he was a former deputy state attorney general. He was also a former Tammany appointee as deputy commissioner in two New York City departments, Markets and Docks. An ordained rabbi, Buchler had also been a chaplain at Sing Sing prison. And in 1922 he had been acquitted of federal perjury charges.

Now Buchler confirmed that he had met on August 5— the day before Crater was last seen—with a woman who introduced herself as "Lorraine Fay." Ms. "Fay" told Buchler, in his capacity as attorney, that she wanted to sue Joseph Crater for $100,000 for "breach of promise," saying that she had compromising letters from him to bolster her case.

Buchler described "Fay" as about thirty years old and said she had been staying for a single night in a hotel off Madison Avenue in the Sixties. (The *World* quickly checked all such hotels and found that no one had been registered at any of them on August 5 under the name Lorraine Fay.) Buchler told the *World* that "Fay" was "a light-complexioned blonde, 5 feet 10 inches tall, between 31 and 35 years old, and weighing about 160 pounds. She had 'thin legs' under a substantial frame and was dressed in a light blue dress."

He described her to that afternoon's *Sun* as having a "beery voice" and said she was "an 'American Jewess,' well dressed and liberally adorned with jewels. He said she spoke good English, but she gave him the impression of being vulgar."

Buchler's account was not entirely consistent, however. On the one hand, he said that he never saw his client again; on the other, he told at least one newspaper that she did, as the letter said, later receive a $5,000 settlement. Having divulged quite a few of his would-be client's confidences, he refused to answer some other questions on grounds of attorney-client privilege.

Most remarkably, Buchler, on reviewing the anonymous letter to the *World*, later testified that the "L. R." referred to was actually "L. B." How he could possibly have known this he never said—and was never asked. But the numerous legalistic phrasings in the letter—"confidential communication," "inasmuch," and "complainant," the references to "Justice" rather than "Judge" Crater—strongly hint that the author had legal training. It seems entirely possible that Buchler wrote the letter himself.

☐   But even if the "Lorraine Fay" letter was a bizarre self-promotional stunt, it did serve to uncover an important figure in the Crater case.

On September 19, the day after the *World* published its initial account of the letter, the *Sun* said that Miss "Fay" matched the description of Constance Braemer Marcus. Marcus was yet another woman with whom Crater had been linked—and the police had been looking for her for days.

Unlike Sally Lou Ritz, Elaine Dawn, and Alice Woods, Connie Marcus did not wish to be found—at least not yet.

On September 13, just three days after the first newspaper reports on some of the other women in Joe Crater's life, Marcus—later described by Stella as a "cloak model and saleswoman"—quit her job at the Maurice Mendel dress shop on East Fifty-seventh Street. At the same time she gave up her apartment in the Hotel Mayflower and left town. She would remain in hiding for nearly two weeks, staying first at a hotel in Norwich, Connecticut, then with a sister in Memphis.

When she did return, Marcus explained to the NYPD and District Attorney Crain that her relationship with Crater had differed markedly from that he had with the showgirls. The police were not surprised. As police Captain John Ayers, commander of the department's Missing Persons Bureau, wrote just a couple of years later in the opening pages of his book *Missing Men*,

> When the wife of a missing man tells us: "Joe and I were ideally happy; we never had a single quarrel," we must take her declaration with a grain of salt and a spice of suspicion. Experience has taught us that Joe, who is so "happily married" to Maud, frequently has a red-headed enchantress just around the corner.

In the case of this particular "Joe," the "enchantress" was described this way:

> a raven-haired modish woman in her mid-thirties. Energetic and vivacious, Constance Marcus had in 1922 [or 1923] been a diligent worker for the Cayuga Democratic Club. She had met Joe Crater while engaged in ringing doorbells during an

election campaign. She liked him and retained him—as had Mrs. Crater—in the matter of her divorce.

"I can't remember his ever having done anything like wooing me," she liked to say. "It just seemed natural and inevitable to us. I honestly feel like a wife."

Marcus's husband was in the federal prison in Atlanta, serving a term for bankruptcy fraud, when she and Crater met. He did not take her divorce case, but by 1924 he was sending her monthly checks, paying "only that portion of the rent which his paramour's income couldn't meet." This practice continued until Crater's disappearance. In fact, Crater mailed a check for $90 from Belgrade Lakes to Marcus in New York sometime on Saturday, August 2. They saw each other often, although Marcus said their last encounter had been on July 24, and that she had not expected to see Crater again until late August. On Crater and Marcus's last evening together they had gone to the theater—to *Artists and Models*.

☐   The Connie Marcus angle was vigorously pursued by investigators, but while titillating, it did not seem to prove enlightening. On September 20 the *Sun* asked if this might not be a coincidence: might the "showgirl" and "mistress" stories be an attempt to distract the public from the real Crater mystery, namely the ties to the Ewald–Healy matter and the broader question of Tammany corruption? After all, the special grand jury that had begun inquiring into the Ewald–Healy affair had returned indictments where Crain had thought none warranted—and had reached this conclusion in just a week.

Such questions about Judge Crater could better be posed
to witnesses like Robert Wagner than to those like Connie
Marcus. On the same day that he said that Stella Crater
might be a suspect in her husband's disappearance, District
Attorney Crain called Senator Wagner to testify. The senator was on the witness stand for ten minutes.

Chapter Six

NEVER
TO BE SEEN
AGAIN

☐   The financial writer John Brooks observed that October 1930 was "the month apple-sellers became prevalent on American street corners." It was also the month in which the disappearance of Joseph Crater and the burgeoning scandals of Tammany Hall began to merge.

On September 5, just two days after the first public report of Crater's disappearance, special investigator Hiram Todd indicated that he would like to see Crater testify in the Ewald–Healy inquiry. But it was not until September 23 that Samuel Seabury moved to broaden the scope of his investigation of the Magistrates' Courts to include attorneys practicing in those courts as well as the magistrates themselves.

Tammany and its officials moved immediately to resist Todd and Seabury's separate forays, as district leaders paraded before Todd's grand jury refusing to waive immunity from prosecution—and, lacking immunity, invoking their rights against self-incrimination. With his bid for reelection just six weeks ahead, and the state Democratic convention set to open and make his renomination official, Governor Roosevelt found himself in a very difficult situation. On one side stood Tammany, whose support could prove important in a close election, now or in 1932. On the other stood an increasingly disquieted public—and Tammany's implacable enemy Seabury.

Roosevelt quickly went public with a request that the leaders testify without immunity. By the first day of October, Roosevelt's pressure had gotten to Jimmy Walker, and the mayor insisted that all district leaders would now face a choice between waiving immunity and resignation from government.

The grand jury before which they were now to testify was Todd's, but the largest impetus for the investigation came from the public hearings Seabury convened in his capacity as "referee." Despite not having been a judge for fourteen years, Seabury appeared at the first such hearing in full judicial regalia, as described by an observer at the scene:

> The buzz of conversation ended abruptly as the door to the referee's chambers opened and Judge Seabury . . . entered the room and briskly mounted the dais. He made an amazingly imposing figure. The black silken folds of the robe set off by contrast a face benign and seemingly out of place on that

bench where a Tammany justice so often sat. His hair was snow-white and as usual parted precisely in the middle. His brown eyes flashed and roved restlessly through the room. In his face were the lines of wisdom and of experience, of patience and of indomitable courage, and about his lips the mobile muscles played, ready to flash a smile or to set in the stern lines of that unwavering justice which his whole appearance symbolized. He looked as a judge should look.

But he was not acting as a judge. The ferocity of Seabury's challenge to Tammany came from the fact that he maintained the control over the proceedings usually reserved to a judge while actually performing the role of a prosecutor, a contestant in the very scene he looked to be "judging."

☐ The Crater investigation, meanwhile, continued to be marked by "sightings" of the missing man. In the rush to be first to solve the mystery, no New York newspaper was immune from such overheated stories. On September 14, as NYPD detectives continued to look for Crater in the Adirondacks in the north and in Southampton on Long Island's eastern end, the *Times* placed Crater in Texas Guinan's Long Island roadhouse two days after his disappearance.

Two days later the *Daily News* had a witness claiming to have seen him sail for the West Indies a week later than that. A waitress in Augusta, Maine, recalled serving Crater and his chauffeur on August 9, when the events she recalled had clearly occurred on July 29. A woman in Phillipsburg, New Jersey, who had known Crater slightly many years earlier, insisted that he had visited her pharmacy on August 8 and stuck to her story when it became clear to everyone else that the visitor had been Crater's cousin Everett. On October 5 a notice mistakenly appeared in the *New York Law Journal* stating that Judge Crater would preside at a trial term of the Supreme Court scheduled to convene the next day.

Each of these reports received some attention; many lingered for weeks, sometimes for years, even though none had any substance. Questions continued to be posed about trivial details of the Crater case, even as central issues remained unexplored. Thus, for instance, as early as October 4, Crain was reported to be preparing a second set of questions for Stella Crater, but he couldn't seem to get around to delivering them.

Nor was this merely a matter of solicitude for the grieving wife. One question that Crain was supposedly eager to pose to Stella was who had called the judge in Belgrade Lakes on the evening of August 3, hastening his return to New York—or, if he had placed the call, to whom it had been made. But, as the *Sun* noted, Crain not only failed to pose this question to Stella, he also did not ask such prospects (suspects?) as Martin Healy or George Ewald if they had been the ones to speak with Crater that night. Nor did he pose this question to anyone else—such as Simon Rifkind.

☐ One germane subject that did receive attention was Crater's finances.

From the first, the best evidence that Crater had vanished voluntarily rather than involuntarily had been the $5,150 in checks he had cashed on the last morning before he disappeared. No one has ever been able to say for certain what that money was intended for. But one of Crater's earlier needs for cash may be more easily explained.

The Ewalds had allegedly made two payments to Healy, totaling $10,000, after Ewald had been named to a judicial post (as a magistrate) paying $12,000 per year. The going rate for judgeships in Manhattan, it was said, was roughly one times the job's annual salary.

Crater's Supreme Court appointment was bigger game. After an increase from $22,500 approved in Albany in 1929, it paid $25,000, the same annual salary received by Governor Roosevelt (and equivalent to $265,000 today). Federal district judges were paid only $10,000 in 1930, and state Supreme Court justices upstate received only $15,000, but New York City provided a $10,000 annual supplement to the $15,000 appropriated by the state legislature. Tammany had made the Supreme Court posts the largest plums on offer.

Investigation now revealed that Crater had been raising a substantial amount of cash just weeks after his appointment to the bench.

On May 23 or 24, 1930, six weeks after his nomination by Roosevelt had been engineered by Wagner, the newly minted judge had opened a brokerage account with Arthur McCabe, a stockbroker who lived on the same floor as the Craters at 40 Fifth Avenue. Why Crater sought to open the account when he already had at least one open brokerage account at Dyer, Hudson & Company is not clear.

Within three days, Crater was using his new account with McCabe to sell shares totaling just over $15,500 ($15,779 to be exact), and immediately turning the proceeds into cash. The stock sales included odd lots of shares in companies ranging from General Electric to United Gas, Chrysler, Montgomery Ward, Standard Oil of New Jersey, International

Telephone & Telegraph, International Paper, Columbia Carbon, and Electric Bond & Share.

All the stock sales were executed by McCabe on May 26. The next morning Crater dispatched Joseph Mara, the confidential assistant he had hired just a month earlier, with a note to McCabe's office to collect $15,000 of the proceeds in cash—specifying that he would like the money in thousand-dollar bills. McCabe, unfamiliar with Mara, insisted on accompanying him back to Crater's chambers, where the money was paid over in exchange for Crater's signed receipt. (The much smaller balance was paid by McCabe, through Mara, in two installments, the following day and one week later.)

On the same day McCabe was counting out fifteen thousand-dollar bills in Crater's chambers, the judge also sent Mara to two banks for large sums of cash. Crater had recently deposited a check for $6,500 for legal fees from Mutual Insurance to an account he had at the International Germanic Trust Company (FDR had been one of this bank's original financial backers.) Now Crater nearly emptied that account, having Mara withdraw $7,000, again in thousand-dollar bills. Mara's rounds also took him to the Chase Bank, from which he withdrew a single five-hundred-dollar bill.

Total cash haul for this one day, May 27: $22,500. Until just a few months earlier, that had been the annual salary of a Supreme Court Justice in New York County.

When these transactions came to light in October, the *Times* quoted "a man associated with Crater in law for a number of years before Crater became a judge"—in other words, either Rifkind or Francis Quillinan—as saying, ". . . if there was any bartering of offices going on Joe Crater was in the know. I don't mean by that that Crater himself bought office but he was in so close with politics that if there was office buying he was aware that it was going on."

Here, of course, was a reason some people might not want the judge found.

On the day after that quote appeared in the *Times*, Republican gubernatorial nominee Charles Tuttle turned the obvious conclusion into a public accusation: Crater's May cash-raising, he alleged, was a payoff for the judicial post he had received from Franklin Roosevelt. Tuttle continued to press his charge the next day, and Walter Lippmann in the *World* took up the cry, suggesting that FDR's nominations of Crater and of Amadeo Bertini to the Court of General Sessions were "enveloped in mystery." Having pressed just a month earlier for a county grand jury to investigate Crater's fate, Lippmann and the *World* now warned that the investigation should not be left to District Attorney Crain.

By October 9, just as Seabury was beginning his own first private hearings, Roosevelt felt compelled to respond. In a letter to State Attorney General Hamilton Ward, FDR wrote that he had nominated Crater after receiving his name as one of eight put forward by the Association of the Bar and one of several endorsed by Tammany. That indicated, he claimed, that "no one sought to bring about" his choice.

To call this disingenuous is more than even Franklin Roosevelt deserves. As Roosevelt must have known, all the names on the original Bar Association list of seven (not eight) candidates had been Jews. And the association committee had made plain its preference for Bernard Shientag, whom FDR had later named to another vacancy on the same court. Even Tammany's first choice had been a Jew.

Most astonishingly brazen was Roosevelt's statement that "no one had sought to bring about" the choice of Crater. What, then, had Senator Wagner been doing at the executive mansion in Albany two days before Crater's nomination was announced?

Perhaps Roosevelt, always careful with words, would have said that Wagner was not foisting the choice of Crater on him—"seeking to bring it about"—so much as simply helping his governor out of a difficult political situation— offering it as a possibility. No matter the semantics, the truly masterful nature of FDR's statement was not in what it appeared to deny but in what it managed to ignore completely. Even taking the governor at his word, that he merely found Crater at the intersection of two enlarged lists of names, the statement does not put Roosevelt on record as to how Crater's name was actually selected. It was a question Roosevelt seems never again to have been asked—and certainly never to have answered.

Roosevelt, of course, was not the only one seeking distance from the decision to place Crater on the bench. The city Bar Association president, C. C. Burlingham, said that Crater had earlier "had the reputation of a man of exceptional ability. . . . I must say I was amazed to find that Mr. Crater had been living such a wretched loose life."

☐　Crain's investigation, meanwhile, continued with its distractions. Roosevelt was never called to testify or to offer documents. But Crain did obtain a court order to force open Judge Crater's safe-deposit box at Empire Safe Deposit, 120 Broadway. After much speculation in the press, the box was pried open—and found empty. And Crain personally took four of the grand jurors on a field trip to the Craters' Fifth Avenue apartment, where they conducted a search of their own. Two earlier searches by NYPD detectives had found nothing of interest, and Crain did not improve on that result.

Judge Crater was supposedly sighted in Phoenix on October 14, and near Los Angeles three days later. In between, with no apparent basis in fact or rumor, Crain mused publicly that Crater might have gone to Havana. The next day, Crain's speculation having produced headlines, the NYPD felt compelled to ask formally for a search by Cuban authorities.

And all of the new focus on money and politics did not entirely sweep away the stories about women. An article in the *Evening Graphic* tabloid on October 11 attributed Crater's disappearance to a "sex urge." The grand jury made another field trip, this one to Polyclinic Hospital, to interview Elaine Dawn. A few weeks later a search was made at Crater's brother Montague's home in Minot, North Dakota. Montague helpfully observed in a letter to Crain that Stella Crater should be "made to talk," although he did not mention that he had not seen his brother in seven years. And Crain continued to assert that he was determined to secure Stella's sworn testimony.

But Crain's means were plainly inadequate to his stated ends. Instead of pressing Maine authorities, with their subpoena power, to pursue the investigation they had seemingly dropped at the first sign of Stella's unwillingness to cooperate, Crain instead sent her a letter. The letter, dated October 15, asked her to come to New York on October 31 to testify before the grand jury. Crain asked Stella to regard the letter "in the light of a subpoena." Which is to say, "I don't have the power to make you attend, but I hope you'll ignore that and feel compelled anyway."

Stella wasn't about to cooperate. As she later wrote,

> Physically, I was in no condition to appear before any such panel of inquisitors. Neither did I intend to be humiliated by being cross-examined concerning Joe's alleged "love affairs." No matter what the cost, I decided with unshakeable determination, I would be the last one to help them assassinate his character and reputation.

Of course, in taking this position she also became the last person to cooperate with the investigation of his disappearance—the last person to help find him. On October 20, Stella and her mother moved out of the summer home in Belgrade Lakes and installed themselves for the winter in a hotel in nearby Portland, still safely beyond the range of Crain's subpoenas. Money was beginning to pinch, so Stella discharged chauffeur Fred Kahler, giving him the family Cadillac in lieu of his unpaid wages. But enough money remained to pay the hotel bill—even as Stella's apartment sat empty in New York City.

☐ On October 19 the *Herald Tribune*, the leading Republican newspaper in New York, published a major investigative piece placing the Crater investigation in the larger context of the ongoing judicial corruption probes.

The newspaper's account reached back to La Guardia's 1929 campaign charges against Magistrate Vitale, the dinner-robbery fiasco a month later, and Vitale's subsequent removal from the bench. Next to fall, it noted, was County Judge W. Bernard Vause, indicted in a pier-leasing scheme by federal prosecutor Charles Tuttle—now, a year later, FDR's Republican opponent in the gubernatorial contest.

Tuttle's investigation of a stock swindle involving Cotter Butte Mining Corporation soon became transformed into yet another tale of judicial corruption. Both district leader Martin Healy and Magistrate George Ewald were officers of Cotter Butte. First Tuttle revealed that Ewald had apparently obtained and sold now-worthless stock in the mining firm in exchange for lenient treatment of a criminal defendant in his court. But when Tuttle referred the matter for prosecution to Crain in May 1930, no action was taken.

Tuttle, however, refused to drop the matter, and soon developed the information that Ewald appeared to have purchased his judgeship from Healy through the good offices of sheriff's clerk Thomas Tommaney. Magistrate and Mrs. Ewald eventually had no choice but to invoke their rights against self-incrimination, and again the matter was referred to Crain, who again failed to act. Roosevelt now felt sufficient pressure that he ordered State Attorney General Ward to continue investigating the matter; he directed that a special grand jury be convened before Supreme Court Justice Philip McCook, a Republican, but limited the inquiry to the Ewald–Healy judgeship-selling allegations. And Samuel Seabury was named by the Appellate Division to launch his inquiry into the Magistrates' Courts.

That is where matters stood when Joseph Crater's disappearance came to public attention.

It was a turning point, as the scope of investigations widened and the level of suspiciousness rose: McCook told the Ewald–Healy grand jurors that they need not confine themselves to the Ewald case, and FDR himself was challenged on his selection of not just Crater but also General Sessions Judge Amedeo Bertini, an unknown lawyer rated as unfit for the bench by at least one of the local bar associations.

Following the repeated headlines on Crater, the opening of the Seabury inquiry, and the early stirrings of FDR's re-election campaign, McCook's "suggestion could not have been better timed for persuasive effect upon the jury and the public."

Senator Wagner, campaigning for Roosevelt, felt compelled to say, "I know that I speak for the heart and conscience of the great rank of the Democratic party in our State when I say that he who attains judicial or public office by dishonest means should be driven therefrom, as also from the ranks of our party."

The candidate himself seemed angry:

> If there are corrupt judges still sitting in our courts they shall be removed. They shall be removed by constitutional process, not by inquisition; not by trial in the press but by trial as provided by law. If there is corruption in our courts I will use every rightful power of the office of Governor to drive it out, and I will do this regardless of whether or not it affects or may affect any Democratic or Republican organization in any one of the five counties of New York City, or any of the other fifty-seven other counties in the State. That is clear. That is unequivocal. That is simple honesty. That is justice. That is American. That is right.

Scrutiny of Bertini's nomination revealed that it appeared to have been engineered by Charles Kohler, who doubled as Mayor Walker's budget director and as a Tammany district leader. But Roosevelt insisted that Bertini had been foisted on him by former State Assembly leader Maurice Bloch; Bloch had since, conveniently, died.

Bertini, called to testify, refused to do so even after a proffer of immunity, as did a raft of Tammany leaders. But, as we have seen, that brought huge criticism down on Walker (including from Roosevelt), and the Tammany leaders agreed to answer questions.

Of all of these inquiries, the *Herald Tribune* survey observed, "the most unusual" was that surrounding Crater:

> It is generally believed that he fled to escape the scandals which have since broken around the activities of the Tammany district organization which he headed. In the inner circles of Tammany it is said that Crater was one of the two real leaders of the 19th Assembly District. Healy is said to be only leader in name.

Whatever the accuracy of this last bit of speculation (and it does not appear to have been on the mark), the key fact about the *Herald Tribune* narrative is that it publicly wove all these events into a larger tapestry, with judicial corruption as the visible thread and Joseph Crater's disappearance as the focal point.

☐ But none of this was sufficient to change the political dynamic of the moment. On November 4, FDR, who had been elected to his first term as governor in 1928 by just 25,000 votes, was overwhelmingly reelected to a second term. The margin of victory this time was more than 725,000 votes. Roosevelt became the first Democratic candidate for governor in the twentieth century to register a plurality outside New York City. Inside the city, Roosevelt outpolled Al Smith's performance in 1926 and Jimmy Walker's in the 1929 race against La Guardia for mayor. Will Rogers summed up the implication in his newspaper column the next morning. "The Democrats," he wrote, "nominated their President yesterday, Franklin D. Roosevelt."

☐ The Crater grand jury, however, was well and truly stymied. On November 7, the Friday following FDR's reelection, the grand jury issued a 16-page preliminary report while transmitting 975 pages of testimony to the court and the NYPD. The conclusion to the preliminary report was at least frank: "The evidence is insufficient to warrant any expression of opinion as to whether Crater is alive or dead or as to whether he absented himself voluntarily or is a sufferer from disease in the nature of amnesia, or the victim of a crime."

One shred of hope was held out: the grand jury would remain on call until January 8, 1931, in case further evidence surfaced. And new witnesses began to be heard almost immediately, with Crater's father appearing to testify the following Tuesday.

But Frank Crater had little to add to the record. His last visit with his son had been from July 20 to 22, when he had come to New York from his home in Orlando, Florida. Joe had taken him to lunch with Martin Healy and had stopped by Mayor Walker's office with his father in tow, although Walker had been out at the time. Finally they had ended up at the Cayuga Club. Frank clearly knew more about his son's political activities than Stella claimed to know, but he was convincing when he said he had no idea where his son had later gone, or with whom.

Stella, meanwhile, remained in Maine, beyond the reach of Crain's subpoenas. On November 18 she spent some time answering an additional forty-five written questions from the district attorney. This time her replies were not released to the public, but it was reliably reported that she continued to insist she had no knowledge of Judge Crater's where-abouts—and certainly no knowledge whatever of Connie Marcus.

With that, the grand jury investigation sputtered to a halt. On January 9, 1931, right on schedule, the grand jury issued its formal report, no different in any respect from the preliminary version it had lodged two months earlier. The grand jurors were discharged. The case of Judge Crater remained a mystery, and while the missing persons file stayed open, no authority in New York City above the rank of police detective was doing anything more to find him.

With no official clue to the whereabouts of her husband, Stella later recalled somewhat oddly, "I felt I could go home to at least a semblance of peace." Within a week, Stella Crater and her mother returned to Manhattan—and to the most surprising developments in the Crater case since the judge's disappearance itself.

☐ Stella Crater's return to New York on January 18, 1931, had been delayed by a few days because her mother, with whom she had been living in Portland, was ill. Stella said publicly at the time that she was returning because the land-lord at 40 Fifth Avenue was threatening to cancel her lease, and because a warehouse wanted payment on her stored fur-niture. In fact, as the foreman of the recently discharged grand jury alleged publicly at the time, and as she later admitted, she was returning as soon as she could—consistent with not having to testify about her husband's disappearance.

The NYPD still had questions for her, of course, and they set her first full day back in town for an interview. But Stella failed to appear. This time she had a good reason.

That morning, she later said, she opened a drawer in a bureau in the bedroom she had shared with her husband, and found four manila envelopes marked with her initials in his handwriting, "SMW personal." The drawer was a sticky one, "unusually formed" and "with a slip over it," normally somewhat obscured from view, and opened with a key that remained lodged in the lock, so that Stella said she had not thought to open it on her August visit home.

The envelopes contained a treasure trove, in a number of senses. Most obvious, no doubt, to Stella was $6,690 in cash, including three thousand-dollar bills, four five-hundred-dollar bills, and fifteen hundred-dollar bills. The *World* soon reported that this included the money the judge had withdrawn from his Chase account on August 6, although it is not clear how this could have been known. The sum, and the denominations, however, made it entirely possible that this was all the money that Crater had withdrawn from both the Chase and Empire Trust accounts that day.

But if the cash was the most obvious haul, it was clearly not the most important. The envelopes also contained $2,600 in checks that Crater had made payable to himself, dated August 30. In addition, they held three endorsed third-party checks, one from Wagner and Rifkind partner (and Al Smith son-in-law) Francis Quillinan for $500, and two from the payment of stock dividends, totaling $21. The most recent of these was dated August 4.

Then there were a miscellany of personal and financial papers, notably including four bank books. (This was before Federal Deposit Insurance, and Crater had at least four open bank accounts at the time of his disappearance, including accounts at the Bowery Savings Bank, the National City Bank, and the Prisco State Bank on Mulbery Street.) And these small accounts were in addition to the Dyer, Hudson brokerage account, where a $5,000 balance remained, net of a $10,000 loan outstanding, and his Empire Trust account, where a $12,000 balance remained—as well as the accounts he had recently closed at the International Germanic Trust, the Manhattan Savings Bank, and the East River Savings Bank.

In all, therefore, and on top of whatever he may have been carrying, it now became clear that Joseph Crater had left behind nearly $25,000 in cash—more than a quarter of a million dollars today—when he disappeared.

Beyond the bank books, the four mysterious envelopes also disgorged Crater's will, dated July 4, 1925 (he left everything to Stella), the lease for the Fifth Avenue co-op apartment, the deed for the Belgrade Lakes house and some property the Craters owned in Florida, their share certificate in the Larchmont Shore Club, and various stock certificates. Three life insurance policies for a total of more than $25,000 had been known to investigators since bills for unpaid premiums had been found in the Craters' unopened mail in October, but now Stella found a fourth policy as well, and the total insured amount climbed to $30,000. No wonder Crater's safe deposit box had been empty when opened.

The last enclosure was by far the most significant. It was a note to Stella, written by her husband in pencil on three sheets of foolscap. Opening with the word "Confidential," but without salutation or date, it consisted almost entirely of a list of people whom Crater asserted owed him money, along with instructions to his wife about how to collect. Twenty-one separate debts were laid out; most did not specify the amounts due, but those that did came to more than $20,000 in the aggregate. Some of the debts were commercial—for legal and other fees past due. Others were of origins less clear, and perhaps of more dubious legality. When the list became public, as it soon did, some of the debts were acknowledged by the individuals named, including four by Francis Quillinan, Senator Wagner and Simon Rifkind's law partner, and one for $1,000 by Reginald Issacs, the lawyer with whom Crater had met at about 5:30 on the afternoon he disappeared. Others were denied.

☐ The third and fourth items on the list of debts concerned the Libby Hotel.

The Libby, a twelve-story brick building located on Delancey at Chrystie Street, was strictly kosher and known as the "Jewish Ritz." It had been completed in 1926 but immediately fell behind on tax payments. After three increasingly precarious years, even as New York's economy boomed around it, the Libby added bond payments to the list of obligations it was not meeting—whereupon Irving Trust foreclosed. The shareholders lost $350,000.

At this point in his legal career, Crater was making quite a business as a receiver of failing properties in the Bronx and

Manhattan. (Receivers manage failing properties or companies. They are appointed by judges, are supposed to maximize the value of assets, and often share in the gains they produce.) All these appointments came Crater's way through friendly judges, many of them from future colleagues such as Alfred Frankenthaler and Louis Valente. In February 1929, Justice Aaron Levy named Crater as receiver of the Libby.

It was all very cozy. Levy later recalled that he made the appointment on the recommendation of someone associated with the American Bond and Mortgage Company, perhaps Crater's friend Martin Lippman. Quilliman was named as referee of the receivership, while Crater named George Frankenthaler, brother of the justice, as attorney for the receiver.

In his capacity as receiver of the Libby, Crater moved swiftly. Within four months he sold the property to the American Mortgage Loan Company, a subsidiary of American Bond and Mortgage. The sale price was $75,000.

But the sale came just ahead of a scheduled Board of Estimate approval of a street-widening project in the area of the hotel. Six weeks after the sale, the City of New York moved to seize the land under the building for the street widening, and condemned the Libby. The price, however, was a far cry from $75,000. Instead, two appraisals now valued the Libby at $1.1 and $1.2 million, while American Mortgage Loan pegged it at $3.105 million. The condemnation award was $2.85 million—a 3,800 percent return for American Mortgage Loan on its investment in just six weeks.

Moreover, it later appeared, Crater's role in all of this did not end when, as receiver, he sold the Libby. Accompanied by former city comptroller Charles Craig, Crater later called on incumbent comptroller Charles Berry and sought to persuade him to have the city purchase the Libby for $3 million—in other words, essentially to split the difference between the proposed award and American Mortgage Loan's asking price.

By the summer of 1930, with the condemnation award not yet paid, an investigation of the Libby transactions was begun, with Leonard Wallstein of the Citizens Union named by Craig as special corporation counsel for the purpose. Wallstein privately notified Craig on July 3, 1930, that he considered the award excessive; Craig soon responded that he agreed. In a letter dated July 23, Wallstein wrote Mayor Walker that he would challenge the condemnation in court.

Stella Crater later recalled discussing this investigation with her husband, and his reassuring her about the propriety of his conduct. This reassurance is curious because the subject did not reach public notice until September 4—four weeks after Judge Crater disappeared, and the day after his disappearance was itself first reported publicly. One possible explanation is that news of Wallstein's challenge was what brought Crater suddenly back from Belgrade Lakes to New York on August 3.

In the note Stella found in the bureau drawer, Crater asserted that he was due "a large sum for my commissions when accounts are passed" and "a very large sum" "for services when the city pays the $2\frac{1}{4}$ million in condemnation." George Frankenthaler was, he wrote, attorney for the receiver in the first matter; as for the "very large sum," "Martin Lippman will attend to it."

☐ When he had concluded his list of debts, Crater was nearly done. He signed the note "Love, Joe," in a clear hand. Then he wrote at the bottom left-hand side of the sheet,

"This is all confidential," underlining the thought—and ending his letter with the same word with which he had begun it.

But before the "Love, Joe," and following the final "He will pay you," were three key words. They are very hard to decipher—far less clear than most of Crater's scrawl. And the last of the three words betrayed either a slip of the hand or a second thought about what to say. The three words are most often read as "Am very weary," and that is the way Stella and the newspapers read them at the time. They could also be read as "I'm very sorry."

☐ Stella Crater found the four envelopes in the bureau on January 19, 1931. In 1939, in a probate proceeding, she testified under oath that she had notified District Attorney Crain "immediately" of her discovery. In a later account she wrote that she did so "as soon as I recovered from my shock." In fact, the first person she and her mother told of this discovery was Stella's attorney, and they waited a day to do that. The attorney then moved quickly to call Crain, who came immediately to the Fifth Avenue apartment in person to take possession of the papers.

Crain made the discovery public and was instantly confronted with questions about why the envelopes had not been found earlier. Police detectives had, after all, searched the apartment on September 4 and September 8—and Leo Lowenthal had been there before that, on August 30 (if not earlier), making an inventory of the judge's belongings. Finally, Crain had taken the grand jurors to the apartment on October 8 on one of their field trips. How had all of these people failed to open the bureau drawer?

The NYPD insisted that they had not failed to do so. Detective Hugh Sheridan, who led the September 8 search, elaborately recalled that it had been a very hot day, and that he had used the key to open that very bureau, found an electric fan inside, and had run it to cool the room as he and his partner conducted their search. But the Craters' friend Garrett Hiers, who used a key given to him by Stella on August 30 to admit the police detectives to the apartment on September 8, directly contradicted Sheridan: the bureau had not been opened, he said.

In 1931 these conflicting accounts were laid out in the newspapers, with reporters seemingly unable to choose between them. What no one seems to have bothered to check was the underlying credibility of Sheridan's story—and it had a fatal flaw: the afternoon high temperature on September 8, 1930 was seventy-two degrees. Perhaps Sheridan had confused his search of September 8 with that led by Detective Edward Fitzgerald on September 4; it is entirely possible that Sheridan joined in that search as well. But the afternoon high on September 4 was only seventy-six.

But even if the police were lying when they said they were certain they had searched that particular bureau drawer, it did not explain how the envelopes had resisted discovery over four searches of the apartment across three months the year earlier. In addressing this mystery within a mystery, what do the contents of the envelopes themselves have to tell us?

First, they place the creation of the package within a relatively tight time frame. As noted, one of the third-party checks was dated August 4; Crater must have prepared the package on or after that date, thus after his return to New York from Belgrade Lakes. The notes about the debts added

146

additional clues; one referred to September 10 in the future tense, one referred in the same manner to September 1. Crain hypothesized publicly, presumably in an attempt to cover for his colleagues in the NYPD, that they must have been placed back in the apartment *after* the September searches, but he failed to take account of this evidence.

So the envelopes were prepared in August, and in New York. That makes it overwhelmingly likely that they were prepared in advance of Judge Crater's disappearance—and makes it highly possible that the money he drew that day was not intended to provide him with the means for escape but rather to give Stella a means for survival.

But if Crater's package was prepared in August, and left in the apartment, why was it not discovered during the four searches? Perhaps because it wasn't there to be found.

Much of Stella Crater's strange behavior throughout the late summer and fall of 1930 and the winter of 1930–1931 can be explained if we alter a single fact in the tale she later told. That fact is that she found the envelopes her husband left for her not in January, when she made her second visit to their apartment since his disappearance, but in late August, when she made her first such visit. If this was the real sequence of events, much that has been recounted makes sense.

Until that time, even up to her first minutes back in the apartment and the middle-of-the-night phone call to Martin Healy, Stella was frantic to find Joe. But once back in Belgrade Lakes, she steadfastly refused to cooperate with the investigation, pushing—through her actions—for delay where previously she had urged haste. The reason would have been clear: before going through the contents of the envelopes, she would have thought her husband perhaps missing, and possibly as a consequence of his own choice. After going through the envelopes, she would have seen that he had left his cash behind and was therefore presumably not preparing to flee, but had been troubled. And she would fairly soon have concluded that he was probably dead.

Finally, the puzzling phenomenon of four searches failing to find the envelopes would be explained: they were not found by Leo Lowenthal, by Detective Fitzgerald or Detective Sheridan, or by the grand jurors because Stella had already found them and tucked them away somewhere. That would have been simple to do, to put them in a suitcase, take them back to Maine, and later return them to where they had been placed originally—a sticky, semi-hidden drawer—once she came back to New York after the investigation ended.

One question remains, however: If Stella found the package in August, why did she not simply reveal its contents then? Two (or two and a half) possible explanations suggest themselves. First, Stella may simply have panicked at her discovery, and needed time to consider the implications. After all, the last words in her husband's note had been, "*This is all confidential.*" Once she had taken that time, she would have found herself back in Maine and unable to explain the discovery innocently. Indeed, once Crain offered his entirely unsupported suggestion that the judge had returned to Maine and met his end there, Stella might reasonably have concluded that surfacing the envelopes while she was in Maine might have somehow tended to incriminate her.

Relatedly (a half-theory), she might have noted the date on the checks to himself that Crater had written for $2,600. They were dated August 30, the very day Stella, pressed by Leo Lowenthal, returned to Maine—the day after she found the package. Perhaps she took the checks as some hint that Joe would return soon after that date, which would also explain why she took Lowenthal's advice and left town. By the time Crater failed to return, she was in Maine, and subject to the line of reasoning noted just above.

A second, entirely distinct possibility is that something in the envelopes themselves convinced Stella to keep their contents a secret. The most likely such element is Crater's references to the Libby Hotel deal.

This second explanation of why Stella did not come forward is lent greater credence when we consider the timing of her eventual return to New York. Yes, it came after the final grand jury report had seemed to put her beyond the reach of Crain's subpoenas. But it also followed another event, just three days after the grand jury report—the payoff on the $2.85 million Libby condemnation award, the triggering event for what Crater had said would be "a very large sum due me."

☐ If that payoff was Stella's objective, she proved unsuccessful. Martin Lippman, rather predictably, quickly came forward to say that Crater was owed money solely as the receiver for the Libby, and had had nothing to do with its condemnation. While a judge refused yet another attempt to set aside the Libby foreclosure and sale, there would be no "very large sum" paid to any Crater on account of the Libby Hotel. Stella received less than $11,000 for her husband's efforts as receiver. Moreover, the depression soon claimed American Bond and Mortgage, which was seen as insolvent just a few months later, and then found itself under investigation by the U.S. Department of Justice for matters unrelated to the Libby.

On January 30, Stella finally sat for an unsworn one-hundred-minute interview with Crain's investigators. She had made yet another discovery in her apartment the previous day, this one a folder with a collection of newspaper clippings, the most recent from July 10 or 11, before the Craters' final trip together to Quebec. But the questioning yielded nothing, and the clippings do not seem to have excited anyone's interest.

Public confidence in Crain himself was shattered, however. He had followed up his early failure to find Rothstein's killer with an inability to solve the Crater case. And the corruption in the Magistrates' Courts, and elsewhere, just seemed to swirl about him. Within weeks Governor Roosevelt had asked Seabury to take on the additional question of whether the district attorney was fit to continue in office. Some months of examinations ensued, highlighted by one of Crain's deputies testifying that among the district attorney's office's tactics in trying to root out crime had been to paint on an office door a sign with the words "Racketeering Complaints Here." This yielded, the deputy said, 150 such complaints, two indictments, and no trials or convictions. Seabury concluded that Crain was incompetent but probably not corrupt, and proposed to leave the matter there. Crain's failure, his fellow high churchman said, "was not due to any lack of personal effort or ignoble motive." Roosevelt concurred.

☐   The public fascination with the Crater saga wound to a conclusion, even as the other events it had helped trigger accelerated. Stella filed Joe's will four days after her return to

New York, and two days after news of the discovery of the envelopes appeared. Letters of administration of her husband's estate were issued to Stella within two weeks after that. The estate itself was valued at more than $50,000, including cash in five bank accounts totaling $12,000, a brokerage account with a $15,000 balance, four life insurance policies with a face value of $30,000, the Fifth Avenue co-op, fees and salary due the judge, and some Florida real estate.

Stella soon left for Florida in the company of her friends Garrett and Clara Hiers, and found herself a place in West Palm Beach. Her husband, she concluded, had been murdered. And, as she later recounted, "it was all due to politics. . . . I shall never forget how most of Joe's political so-called friends dodged me after his disappearance. This is my main reason for thinking that, if it was anything, it was politics."

☐ Was she right? Certainly "politics" was the reason no one seems to have searched as hard as they might have for Joseph Crater. But murder? Probably not.

The key clues, as all observers of the Crater mystery have intuitively understood since their discovery, lie in the envelopes Stella "discovered" in January 1931. As we have already seen, those envelopes quite possibly contained the cash Crater had Joseph Mara assemble on August 6. Much has been made over the years about the papers he also gathered that day and took from his chambers to his home. But if we allow for some small exaggeration on the parts of Mara and law secretary Frederick Johnson about the quantity of those papers, the envelopes Stella found may explain this as well: both sets of papers may have contained the bank books, insurance policies, stock and share certificates, deeds, cooperative apartment lease, and will that Crater left with his note. Looked at in this light, the only "mysterious" thing Crater did that day in his chambers is to begin assembling the package he left for his wife.

But what, then, became of the judge himself? Clearly he was troubled, under pressure, perhaps even great strain. The checks he wrote to himself and dated August 30 suggest that he may have intended to go somewhere for a few weeks.

It is possible, of course, that he ran away and simply chose never to return, even as his disappearance became national and even global news, and was never spotted, even as hundreds of false sightings of him were reported to authorities. It is also possible that he was the victim of a random or premeditated act of violence, followed by the permanent hiding or destruction of his remains.

But there is also another possibility, involving a young woman named Polly Adler.

☐   Polly Adler was perhaps the leading madam in the New York of 1930.

She was born Pearl Adler in the White Russian town of Yanow, near the Polish border, in 1900, the oldest of nine children. Young Pearl was sent alone to America by her parents at the age of twelve, and lived for two years with friends of friends in Holyoke, Massachusetts. She left there for the home of distant relatives in Brooklyn at the age of fourteen, and went to work in factories. At eighteen she was the victim of what we would now call "date rape" by her supervisor, became pregnant, and had an abortion. By the time she was twenty, she was sharing a room in Manhattan with a woman who introduced her to opium parties.

But Adler, by now known as "Polly" rather than Pearl, was ambitious and strong-willed. She chose commerce over drugs and alcohol, and was set up in her next apartment by a gangster who soon became the backer of her first venture into prostitution, and her first customer as well. Adler was never a prostitute herself, but by 1922 she had amassed $6,000 in savings (about $65,000 today) from her new work. She tried to use this nest egg to fund a lingerie shop, but it failed, and in 1923 she returned to life as a madam.

Through the 1920s Adler's business thrived, and she prospered. She was occasionally raided, and sometimes arrested, but never prosecuted or convicted of anything. She moved from one good Manhattan address to another better one; in 1927 she set up shop in an apartment at Fifty-ninth Street and Madison Avenue. By her own later account, her customers included George McManus (the man who had shot Arnold Rothstein), the owner of one of the American League baseball clubs, a leading boxer, a chain store magnate, the noted writers Robert Benchley and George S. Kaufman, and any number of public officials and other Tammany figures.

That was where the life of Polly Adler stood on August 6, 1930.

Much later, when she had "retired," Adler, with the unacknowledged assistance of the novelist Virginia Faulkner, wrote a memoir, *A House Is Not a Home*, in which this remarkable life is detailed. Meyer Berger of the *New York Times* wrote that "The personal experience story Miss Adler tells—or, more likely, has had someone put down for her—had better have been left unrecorded." But *A House Is Not a Home* became the tenth-best-selling nonfiction work of 1953.

A gossip column–style "blind item" in a 1960 book, however, indicates that there may have been more to Adler's story. One "theory" on Crater's disappearance, it states, had been "already set in type" but "was sliced out of the autobiography of one of New York's celebrated house-is-not-a-home madams." Why the passage would have been excised is not clear, but what it purportedly said is laid out, albeit continuing in the same sort of purple prose:

> "Crater suffered a fatal heart attack at the moment of peak enjoyment while indulging in the unique pleasures of the establishment. Thrown into a state of terror by the demise of such an important man on her premises, the madam appealed hysterically to underworld friends. They removed the body, giving it a full cement-coffin burial in the Hudson River."

Allen Churchill, the author who passed along this "theory" decades ago, dismissed it in his next paragraph on the grounds that it should not have been necessary to make the body disappear. But if Polly Adler did include this account in the manuscript of *A House Is Not a Home*, as it seems Churchill believed she had, this dismissal seems misplaced.

The Adler story squares with all of the evidence in the Crater case. First, Crater's casual relationships with numerous showgirls and his visits to places such as Club Abbey and similar clubs in Atlantic City make clear that frequenting a house of prostitution would hardly have been out of character for him.

Next, this would logically complete the timeline of Crater's activities on the evening of August 6. He might have walked from Billy Haas's restaurant to see the last act of *Dancing Partner* nearby, which would explain both why no taxi driver ever came forward to say that he had picked up Crater in front of the restaurant *and* how the ticket left for him by the Arrow agency *was* picked up. Following the show, Crater might have gone to Club Abbey and from there to Polly Adler's apartment a few blocks away, or directly to Adler's. Perhaps Crater had then intended to slip away for a few days or weeks, or perhaps he simply hadn't yet figured out how to deal with the pressure, or "weariness," he was feeling as the Libby Hotel transaction came under scrutiny and judgeship-buying allegations dominated the front pages.

With respect to the disposal of Crater's body, there is no question that Polly Adler knew men who could have, and would have, attended to this for her. For one, in later years, her leading patron was Dutch Schulz. Adler insists that she did not meet Schulz until June 1931, and that may be so. But even if it is, making a judge who died in the act while investigations of judicial corruption swirled around him literally disappear most certainly would have been in her interest. And, if she had done so, rumors of it would almost certainly have reached Crater's associates, explaining why they quickly concluded that he was dead—and the less investigated, the better.

In the published version of *A House Is Not a Home*, Adler did make one reference to Judge Joseph Crater. In a book of clear sentences and plain meaning, she used an unusual turn of phrase, perhaps one with multiple meanings. Crater, she wrote, was "apparently overmastered by a disinclination to stand up and be counted."

☐   As inquiries into various sorts of corruption intensified in November 1930, Polly Adler received a warning of an impending raid, and then advice that she leave town for a while. She did so, and didn't return until May 1931. The day after she came back to New York she was subpoenaed by Samuel Seabury's investigators. She spent much of a month testifying. Although she steadfastly refused to name her clients, a policeman who had been her silent partner was unmasked and forced to resign from the NYPD. But Adler was back in business by July 1931, and remained so until the end of World War II. Investigators shifted their attention to other matters.

Chapter Seven

TAMMANY

AT THE

VANISHING POINT

☐ The final direct challenge to Tammany came on March 23, 1931, when the state legislature formally initiated an investigation of New York City government. The investigative committee would be chaired by Republican State Senator Samuel Hofstadter. Sixteen days later, Samuel Seabury accepted Governor Roosevelt's suggestion that he be named as counsel to the Hofstadter Committee. Seabury was now conducting three simultaneous inquiries: of the Magistrates' Courts, of District Attorney Crain, and of Jimmy Walker's city government. Throughout 1931, Seabury seemed to be constantly beginning and ending various phases of these investigations. The Crain probe began in March, with hearings starting in April; a final report was submitted in August. The look at the Magistrates' Courts, which had begun the previous August, was concluded by May—just in time for the city investigative hearings to begin in July.

The Magistrates' Courts inquiry produced substantial, tangible results. By the time it concluded, in addition to the earlier removal of Magistrate Vitale as a result of the Rothstein loan, two magistrates had been removed from office and four others had resigned under pressure. Thus eight of the fifty sitting magistrates had been ousted. (The success of the investigation was not unmitigated: George Ewald resigned his judgeship, but two trials of Martin Healy and clerk Thomas Tommaney and one of the Ewalds themselves all ended in hung juries.)

The NYPD vice squad, much of whose work was prosecuted in the Magistrates' Courts, was discovered to be thoroughly corrupt and was abolished. Six police officers were criminally convicted in the vice-squad probe; forty other officers faced lesser charges, twenty-three lawyers who had practiced in the courts were disbarred, and thirty-eight bondsmen who thrived on the proceedings were also charged.

The standard vice-squad scheme was revealed by a Seabury star witness with the wonderful name of Chile Mapocha Acuna, whom the newspapers gave the even more wonderful nickname of "the human spitoona." Acuna explained how he would innocuously talk his way into the apartments or hotel rooms of innocent women, following which vice-squad officers would burst in and arrest the women as prostitutes. Acuna would then testify that the women had solicited him; his role was known as that of the "stool pigeon."

A number of schemes were at work here: some of the arrests were intended to generate legal fees for defense lawyers or fees for bondsmen, who would then kick back a portion of their gain to the arresting officers and often the prosecutors. One prosecutor pleaded guilty to accepting six hundred bribes to bring charges against that many innocent women. In other cases, bribes were solicited and accepted simply to drop the charges. In still other instances, arrests were made solely to fill a quota, often toward the end of a month. Many entirely innocent women went to jail, some for months. Convictions for prostitution also, of course, devastated their reputations with employers, friends, and family.

Acuna was moved to tell this tale by an unusual route. In one case he had been threatened by the husband of an accused woman, who kept a rooming house. At her trial Acuna testified that the defendant was telling the truth: she had not solicited him. The woman was acquitted, but the arresting officer, infuriated, now turned on Acuna and arrested him for attempted extortion of the woman. Acuna was sent to prison for a year; when he was released he went straight to Seabury.

Much skepticism attended Acuna's charges, but the police had underestimated him. Acuna had kept detailed written records of each of eighty-two frame-ups in which he had been involved. And at hearings before Seabury one day, with most of the members of the vice squad having been compelled to attend, he walked through the audience, touching twenty-seven different NYPD officers on the shoulder, and calling each one by name as he did so. He made only one mistake, calling a twenty-eighth officer by the name of his partner.

While much of the corruption in the Magistrates' Courts was tragic, some was also comic. Magistrate Jean Norris changed court transcripts to cover up her trampling on the rights of defendants. But she also was sanctioned for accepting $1,000 to allow her picture to be placed in an advertisement that contained a letter from her endorsing the digestive value of Fleischmann's Yeast. Norris, New York's only female judge, had refused a $500 offer for the endorsement, insisting on the larger figure. Just as it had with Vitale, the Appellate Division removed her from office.

The Magistrates' Courts inquiry also produced one sidelight to the Crater case, about which speculation still lingers. On February 26, 1931, a young woman named Vivian Gordon was found strangled in Van Cortlandt Park in the Bronx. Gordon had been a prostitute, a competitor of Polly Adler's, and had just begun cooperating with Seabury's inquiry into the vice squad—largely as a way to retaliate against the police officer who had helped send her to prison for three years in 1923. Gordon's case became a tabloid *cause célèbre*, particularly after her sixteen-year-old daughter committed suicide a week later. The *New York Daily News* in 1931 and a magazine called the *American Weekly* in 1956 attempted to link Gordon's murder to the notion that Crater was also murdered. But the key in this chain of illogic was a visit Crater ostensibly made to Sing Sing prison three weeks after his disappearance. It is clear from prison records, and has been since 1931, that no such visit took place; Gordon appears to have been murdered for her mink coat. Her murderer was acquitted but was executed in 1955 for another crime. The only true link between Gordon and Crater may have been more pedestrian.

The man who later murdered her, Harry Stein, said that he had once met Crater at Gordon's apartment.

☐   When Seabury turned his attention from the Magistrates' Courts to the larger issues of city government, attention returned to "Horse Doctor" Doyle, the Fire Department veterinarian who had been on trial the day Judge Crater disappeared. Doyle had been acquitted and still had not revealed with whom he had been splitting the large fees for his remunerative work before the city's Board of Standards and Appeals. Seabury issued a subpoena for Doyle to appear before him as a witness. Doyle fled beyond the reach of the subpoena to New Jersey, but was returned to New York after federal prosecutors indicted him on charges of income tax evasion. Duly served with the subpoena by Seabury, only one question was posed to him: "Are you going to tell me with whom you split your fees?"

Doyle refused to answer and was held in contempt. The seriousness of the threat such inquiries were beginning to pose to Tammany became evident when Grand Sachem John Curry himself intervened, calling a justice of the Appellate Division on vacation in Lake Placid to get Doyle's contempt citation quashed. Curry's effort to stop what he later called an attempt at "a crucification . . . of the Democratic party of the City of New York" backfired when it soon became public knowledge, but Doyle steadfastly refused to answer.

The comparisons of (relatively small) salary with (enormously large) income that had proven so illuminating with Doctor Doyle, however, now became a key weapon in

Seabury's arsenal. The register of Kings County, Seabury showed, had deposited $520,000 (more than $6 million today) in six years; he said he had borrowed it from a series of friends and associates but couldn't remember exactly who, and had kept no records. The deputy city clerk in charge of marriage licenses rang up just under $385,000 (about $4.5 million today) in seven years; he said that about $150,000 came from "tips" from happy grooms, but expressed surprise that there had been so much more, and couldn't account for it. The former sheriff of New York County had banked just under $2 million (nearly $21 million in today's value) over seven years.

The Democratic boss of Queens had gotten a man he had installed as surrogate to, in turn, give him an $8,000-per-year job as chief clerk in that court. The boss explained a suspicious $15,000 deposit by saying that he had long had the cash lying around his home. Most of it, he said, had come from a winning bet at a Florida race track. "I kept the money in my desk, sometimes," he said, "and sometimes I kept it down cellar. It was in a box. It was in a tin box."

Which brought Seabury to the incumbent sheriff of New York County, Thomas Farley. Farley was the Tammany leader on the East Side, where he had been born and brought up. At thirteen he had left school to work as a wagon boy for Bloomingdale's. From there he moved on to become business agent for the Cement and Concrete Workers' Union. In 1915, at the age of twenty-seven, he was elected to the Board of Aldermen, where he served eight years. He then became deputy city clerk, and in 1930 was elected sheriff.

Over seven years, from 1925 through late 1931, Seabury showed, Farley had earned just over $53,000. But he had deposited in various accounts more than $360,000, or roughly $4.3 million today. His testimony in explanation was classic:

> "It represented moneys I had saved. I took the money out of the safe deposit at home."
> "Where did you keep the cash?"
> "In a big safe."
> "But in a little box in a big safe?"
> "In a big box in a big safe." . . .
> "And Sheriff, was this big box that was safely kept in the big safe a tin box or a wooden box?"
> "A tin box."
>
> . . .
>
> "Well, then, we come to 1928. That year you deposited $58,177.75. Where did you get that money, Sheriff?"
> "That was moneys the same way."
> "You mean?"
> "I mean it came from the good box I had."
> "Kind of a magic box, wasn't it, Sheriff?"
> "It was a wonderful box."

The public was not amused. Seabury sought Farley's removal by Governor Roosevelt. FDR, working with Columbia professor Raymond Moley (who had also assisted Seabury in the Magistrates' Courts and Crain investigations), formulated a new standard to be applied in such cases:

> . . . when a public official is under inquiry or investigation, especially an elected public official, and it appears that his scale of living, or the total of his bank deposits far exceeds the public salary which he is known to receive, he, the

elected public official, owes a positive public duty to the community to give a reasonable or credible explanation of the sources of the deposits, or the source which enables him to maintain a scale of living beyond the amount of his salary.

Applying this standard to Farley clearly mandated his removal from office, and Roosevelt took that step a week later. The question then became whether the standard would also be applied to the mayor of the city of New York.

☐   For Jimmy Walker, the autumn of Joseph Crater's disappearance proved to be the beginning of the end. At first, Crater's fate didn't seem to touch the mayor. Yes, Stella Crater had made one of her frantic, middle-of-the-night telephone calls to him when she came to town at the end of August, but no one seemed to pursue that fact. When the Crater story went public, Walker turned up with one of his simple, soothing responses—he would offer a reward.

But as the scandals multiplied and deepened, Walker was increasingly pressed to respond. In early October 1930 he was compelled to order Tammany district leaders to waive immunity when testifying before the Seabury and other inquiries, or to resign the public offices that nearly all of them held. By November, Walker himself was recalled for a second round of testimony in the Ewald–Healy investigation. At his first appearance, before District Attorney Crain's regular grand jury, Walker had testified for twenty minutes and departed to applause; this time, before the special state grand jury, he answered questions for a full hour and left to silence.

Walker's messy personal life also took a bad turn. The frantic, devil-may-care quality of his romance with Betty

Compton, which had seemed in keeping with the spirit of the Roaring Twenties, faded as hard times tightened their grip on the city. The fun may have gone out of it for Jimmy and Betty (he called her "Monk") as well; on February 16, 1931, Compton suddenly eloped to Havana with a friend named Edward Dowling. But the marriage to Dowling had been just a vengeful impulse for a spat with Walker, and six weeks later Compton ended her Cuban marriage by filing for a Mexican divorce.

Seabury's broad investigation of Walker's government had barely begun when the Reverend John Haynes Holmes and Rabbi Stephen Wise, acting on behalf of the City Affairs Committee, sought to short-circuit the proceedings. They filed a petition with Governor Roosevelt charging Walker with "incompetent, inefficient and futile conduct" of his office, and asked the governor to invoke his power to remove the mayor from office. Roosevelt formally sought a reply from Walker to the charges—itself something of a rebuke. But then, reply in hand, he refused to order a public hearing on the grounds that the documents submitted by the religious leaders dealt almost entirely with the acts of Walker's subordinates. It was clear, however, that the focus on the mayor was just beginning; one national magazine headlined its summary, "Round One Won by Walker."

The attention shifted to Seabury's hearings under the aegis of the Hofstadter Committee. Through the summer and fall of 1931 these hearings revealed matters such as Farley's tin box. By the spring of 1932 only one target remained: the mayor himself. Roosevelt would not be rushed, however. When Reverend Holmes and Rabbi Wise made another public appeal for him to step in, FDR instead lashed out at them, asserting that if the two preachers "would serve their God as they seek to serve themselves, the people of the City of New York would be the gainers."

Walker defiantly, and triumphantly, led a "beer parade" demanding an end to prohibition down Fifth Avenue on May 14, but the inquiries were not slowed by the parade's proof that his popularity seemed undimmed. The Hoftstadter Committee issued a subpoena to Walker on May 23, and on the 25th he appeared for two days of testimony.

Walker was due to take the witness stand at 11 A.M. Crowds began to assemble outside at 7:00, and every seat in the courtroom was taken within minutes when the doors were mistakenly opened at 8:30. Walker arrived, jauntily decked out all in blue: blue double-breasted suit, blue shirt, blue tie, blue pocket handkerchief, blue socks, blue stone in his pinky ring. He told his valet, "Little Boy Blue is about to blow his horn—or his top." To reporters waiting outside the hotel where he was living, he said, "There are three things a man must do alone. Be born, die, and testify." As he walked up the courthouse steps he encountered a spectator still hoping for a place in the courtroom. "I'd be most happy to give you *my* seat," Walker said.

He was right not to want to be there.

Over the next two days, Seabury led Walker through appalling tales of greed and ignorance. Many had been developed through the earlier testimony of other witnesses, but now it was time for Walker to provide answers, and he had none. The publisher Paul Block, it became clear, in 1927 had opened a joint brokerage account in his name and the mayor's. Walker never put anything into the account, but in its first three months he withdrew $100,000 in cash. By the time the account was closed, with fortuitous timing, in August 1929, Walker had reaped $246,000 ($2.6 million today), after the deduction of income tax payments. Block had testified that he was inspired to do this for Walker after a conversation with his ten-year-old son:

> ". . . the youngster said, 'How much salary does the Mayor get' and I told him $25,000, which was his salary at the time.
>
> 'Does the City give him a home?,' and I said, 'No, they don't.' I recall he said, 'Does it give him an automobile?' And I said, 'Yes, but not to Mrs. Walker.'
>
> 'Well,' this youngster said, 'can he live on what he gets?' And I said, 'Well, I suppose he can, but it probably is a difficult problem.'
>
> And, Judge, I want you to believe me that it entered my mind then that I was going to try to make a little money for him."

Walker insisted that he had been at risk of loss in the account; at the most, he said, monies of this sort were "beneficences" from his friends. The money from Block, he said, had all been placed in a safe—"Not a vault, not a tin box—a safe in my house." It had been "available for Mrs. Walker and myself."

Another subject of testimony was the 1927 award of a bus franchise for crosstown routes in Manhattan and routes in Brooklyn and Queens to the Equitable Bus Company, an enterprise with no experience or financing. On the day before the award was officially signed, a representative of the bus company had paid cash for a $10,000 letter of credit made out in the mayor's name. The day after the signing, the letter of credit was delivered to Walker in person at City Hall. The same representative also later made good on a $3,000 overdraft by Walker.

In 1929, Seabury established, J. A. Sisto, owner of the Checker Cab Company, was seeking municipal legislation to limit the numbers of taxis on the streets. Sisto gave Walker roughly $26,500 in oil company bonds, ostensibly representing Walker's profits in a stock deal. Once again, as with the Block account, the mayor claimed he had been at risk of loss. His only concern in the matter seemed to be his insistence that he had received the bonds in his hotel room rather than while riding in an automobile, as one witness claimed. Taking the bonds in a car, Walker felt, would have been unseemly.

Much of Walker's testimony revolved around bills and records managed for him by Russell Sherwood, his accountant. As Walker said, "I haven't seen a checkbook of my own or a stub or cancelled voucher in six years." That was Sherwood's job, and he seemed to do it extraordinarily well. From 1926, nearly $1 million, $720,000 of it in cash, had moved through a joint checking account and a brokerage account that Sherwood administered. He wrote checks for Allie Walker's yacht and to reimburse Betty Compton for a profit in stock on which she had missed out when the mayor had failed to order a trade. (The prevailing sense of decorum mandated that Compton be referred to throughout the hearings as the "unnamed person.") Despite Walker's testimony, some of the money run by Sherwood appeared to have come from Block while other sums bore all the earmarks of kickbacks as small as $6,000 on a $10,000 salesman's commission on a city street-sweeping contract. Walker may also have benefited directly, as well as indirectly, from the designation of doctors in city workers' compensation cases—the doctors then split their fees with Walker's brother William, also a doctor.

Walker was forced to wade through this detail with Seabury in part because Sherwood would not. Seabury had issued a subpoena for Sherwood in August 1931, but the accountant decamped first to Asbury Park, New Jersey, then to Chicago and finally to Mexico. In October, Seabury served him with a subpoena there, but Sherwood refused to return and was held in contempt of court and fined $50,000. He lost his job at the Manhattan Trust Company but continued to keep Walker's confidences. When Sherwood later returned to the United States, he settled in New Jersey but relied on the inability of the courts to extradite him on a mere contempt charge. He and Walker saw each other again in September 1932, but Sherwood, who lived another twenty-five years, never again entered the jurisdiction of New York. Walker always maintained that he had nothing to do with Sherwood's whereabouts.

The mayor had been greeted in the courtroom on the first day of the hearings with loud applause. Less than thirty-six hours later, the popular perception had changed. The *New York Times* said Walker "left the witness stand trailing clouds, not of glory but of mystery." The *New York Post* went further: "from any standpoint of real intelligence he scored a failure so deep as to make one's flesh creep."

Predictably, Seabury's report to Roosevelt, issued less than two weeks later, recommended Jimmy Walker's removal from office. Now the governor was in a bind.

☐ For years, suspicion of Franklin Roosevelt's willingness to confront Tammany Hall had been a cloud on his presidential ambitions. On the afternoon before his 1930 reelection as governor, for instance, Walter Lippmann had written a scathing editorial in the *Evening World*. Referring to "the Governor's surrender to Tammany on the issue of corruption in this city," Lippmann had written that Roosevelt's

> sacrifice of forthrightness and courage to what seemed to him campaign expediency, has been and still is a profound disappointment. . . .
>
> Had the Governor been firm with Tammany he would have been a far bigger man than he is now in the eyes of state and nation. Even in politics prompt courage is better than courage too obviously delayed for a purpose. He may yet find that out.

By 1932 such doubts were multiplying, even as Roosevelt continued to move toward the Democratic presidential nomination—and, as the depression deepened, likely election. Roosevelt sought to thread a political needle: to show enough independence from Tammany to appeal to a national audience, yet not to antagonize Tammany so much as to cost him New York's votes, either at the Democratic National Convention in Chicago or at the polls in November.

In February, Samuel Seabury could stand this compromising no longer. Seabury had dreamt of the White House for himself in the early years of the Great War, before his betrayal by Tammany and another Roosevelt, and his defeat for governor in 1916. And he would quite possibly have been a strong contender in 1920 or 1924 had he won that election. Now, he and his friends came to believe, the dream might be revived.

On February 26, 1932, just two days after FDR's removal of Farley, Seabury went to Cincinnati to give a speech. He used the occasion to slash into Tammany—but also to try to wound Roosevelt. The facts on Farley, he pointed out, had been brought out months before, and only his own filing of charges had finally moved the matter along. But beyond this, he observed,

> Intoxicated with the absolute power which it possesses in the City of New York, and the great influence which it exerts in the State, Tammany now reaches out to extend its power and use its influence in support of some candidate who will be friendly to it, if, indeed, he does not openly wear the stripes of the Tammany Tiger. . . .
>
> The power of Tammany Hall is not only a menace to New York City—it is a menace to the nation as well.
>
> It drives public men, whose instincts would lead them to speak out in protest against the corruption that has been revealed, to a sullen silence.
>
> They know the conditions are evil, but they fear to antagonize the power of Tammany Hall, and politicians seeking its favors cater to it even when they feel they would be discredited if they openly lined up with it. Where they hold public office and are forced upon given occasions to rule adversely to Tammany Hall, they soften their opposition so that while the public will not regard them as pro-Tammany, Tammany Hall will not regard them as opposed to it

Roosevelt, in other words, was no better than Al Smith. And the man to deliver the nation from this "menace" was Samuel Seabury.

FDR answered Seabury's shrill fury with large measures of calculated silence and delay. Seabury, he was confident, would prove no more attractive as a candidate in 1932 than he had in 1916, and in this Roosevelt calculated correctly.

The Seabury "boom" proved scarcely a boomlet; by the time of the convention in Chicago, the only person who may have taken Seabury's chances seriously was the Judge himself.

Al Smith too finally moved to challenge Roosevelt for the nomination, but his campaign proved a classic political example of too little, too late. Walker made a show of casting his vote as a delegate at the convention for Smith, who said, "Good old Jimsie! Blood is thicker than water!" But the Happy Warrior had long since lost his last serious battle for public office.

Roosevelt had the Democratic nomination, and President Hoover was largely discredited by the depression. Yet the political difficulty for Roosevelt remained as he faced the general election campaign, and Seabury would do nothing to ease FDR's discomfort.

Then Jimmy Walker came to Roosevelt's rescue. The governor carefully and thoroughly prepared himself for hearings he had ordered on Seabury's charges against Walker. Walker, on the other hand, devoted his efforts to obfuscation and attempts, in public appeals and court filings, to obstruct or derail the proceedings. The hearings convened in Albany on August 21, 1932, and lasted five days. Roosevelt was confident in his appearance, composed throughout. He did not hesitate to take over the questioning himself at times, and made rulings (he was serving effectively as both judge and jury) with assurance. Walker again left the witness stand a much smaller figure than he came to it.

Roosevelt retired to weigh the evidence—and to resume preparations for the general election campaign scheduled to begin just days later. One adviser, advocating only a reprimand but realizing that Roosevelt was inclined toward removal and fearing the political consequences for New York's forty-seven electoral votes, snapped at him, "So you'd rather be right than President!" But just as Roosevelt was facing up to the costs and benefits of removing the city's mayor, Walker took two blows that seemed to break him. On August 28, Walker's brother George died in Saranac Lake, New York, after a long illness. The next day Walker's last judicial challenge to Roosevelt's authority to conduct the hearings and, if warranted, to remove him was rejected. Returning from his brother's funeral, and under some pressure from Tammany leaders himself, Walker decided to resign the mayoralty.

In his manner of doing so, Walker likely sealed Franklin Roosevelt's election as president. Walker did this by exploding at Roosevelt. "Instead of an impartial hearing," the mayor said in a public statement accompanying his September 1 resignation, "the proceeding before the Governor developed into a travesty, a mock trial, a proceeding in connection to which even this practice of a drumhead court-martial seems liberal." Alluding to the presidential campaign, Walker, with no trace of the irony involved, alleged conflict of interest, saying that Roosevelt had "a personal interest in the outcome of the pending proceeding. . . . Despite declarations of fairness, he has been studiously unfair."

Beyond New York, this was just the reassurance about Roosevelt and Tammany corruption that many had been seeking. Closer to home, Walker had gone too far for his Tammany

Hall colleagues. Tammany's leaders had perhaps been prepared to "sit on their hands" to allow Roosevelt to be defeated,
just as they had done in 1916 when Seabury ran for governor.
But overt opposition to the Democratic party's nominee for
president could erode discipline, and was not conceivable.
Walker initially declared that he would be a candidate to re-
claim his job, that he was "submitting my case to the people
who made me Mayor," but rather than staying in New York to
campaign he sailed for Europe. Russell Sherwood was among
those seeing him off.

☐   Walker's removal, of course, was not the end of the story.
   By law, the mayoralty devolved on the president of the
Board of Aldermen, Joseph V. McKee. McKee, just forty-
three years old in his seventh year in citywide office (he and
Walker had been elected together in 1925, and reelected in
1929), was a protégé of Ed Flynn and a devout Catholic. He
had earlier earned a doctorate in law from Fordham, taught
English at De Witt Clinton High School, and written a high
school textbook on the European discovery of the Americas
before serving five years in the Assembly and one as a judge
on the City Court.

   McKee had been acting mayor during Walker's many absences from New York, and had already displayed his strait-
laced style when, on one such occasion, he ordered the
closing of two racy plays. He took this step even though one,
The Captive, which dealt with homosexuality, had already
been running some months. In political circles, such moves
earned him the nickname "Holy Joe." He had done nothing
to rock the Walker boat while it remained afloat, but the con-

trast with the deposed mayor was stark. As a contemporary chronicler put it, "Walker slighted his job, and McKee worked at his; Walker bounced out of difficult situations with a wisecrack, and McKee had to struggle out; Walker was bored by the actual business of governing a city, and McKee was fascinated by it."

Voters loved this earnestness, particularly as the depression deepened. Politicians hated it. McKee moved quickly as mayor to cut city expenses and ostentatiously eliminated nearly all the city's chauffeur-driven limousines. But the politicians noted that he retained one for himself—and used it to be deposited at the subway entrance.

The same law that placed McKee in the mayoralty also provided for a special election in November 1932 to fill the last year of Walker's second term. In this race Flynn sought the Democratic nomination for McKee, but the other party leaders would not hear of it—they didn't like McKee and worried that Flynn would gain too much from such a move, at the expense of Tammany. In some still-loyal quarters, a boomlet even developed for Walker, but after toying with the idea he allowed Betty Compton to talk him out of it, and then arranged to be on board a ship from Paris back to New York, and thus safely out of reach, during the October nominating convention. When the ship finally docked, Walker pronounced himself "still a Democrat, though very still." Walker and Compton soon returned to Europe and in April 1933 were married in Cannes.

McKee declined to run as an independent, but he did support a court challenge to the special election itself. When that failed, a write-in campaign was begun on his behalf, although he did not actively promote it.

Tammany turned instead to Surrogate John Patrick O'Brien as its standard-bearer. A thirty-year municipal employee (including service as Mayor Hylan's corporation counsel), O'Brien was stolid, but his honesty was unquestioned. In 1932 it was enough, as he was easily elected, aided significantly by Roosevelt's presidential landslide in New York. But the warning signs were everywhere. O'Brien failed to win a majority of the vote. Roughly 335,000 voters tried to write in the name of McKee, although about 100,000 of these did not fulfill all the legal requirements and their votes were not counted. And O'Brien ran 400,000 votes behind Roosevelt in the city—and 475,000 behind the even greater margin of Herbert Lehman for governor.

As mayor, O'Brien just could not seem to get out of his own way, especially when it came to matters of rhetoric. He went before a Jewish audience and lauded that "scientist of scientists, Albert Weinstein." He told an audience in Harlem that "my heart is as black as yours." He sought to inform Greek Americans that he had spent time in college translating that "great Greek poet, Horace." As reporters looked on, he told an audience of Tammany workers to work for the machine because "Reward will come." When journalists asked who he intended to name police commissioner, he readily confessed, "I don't know. I haven't got the word yet."

The historian Thomas Kessner sums up the situation this way:

> O'Brien was not an idiot. He was a kindly, likable man, intelligent and even witty in private company. He cleared out some redundant city offices, streamlined the Sanitation

Commission, and consolidated several municipal agencies, but he did nothing to clean out the city's patronage nest, and he so closely fit the caricature of the fatuous Tammany politician that few took him seriously.

In 1933, it seemed, the job of mayor might be up for grabs.

☐   That, of course, had been Fiorello La Guardia's plan all along.

La Guardia sat out the unexpected 1932 mayoral campaign for a number of reasons. First, a campaign waged across only two months, from Walker's resignation in early September to early November, played to Tammany's organizational strengths. Second, La Guardia's own congressional reelection effort was already under way. Third, and no doubt most persuasive, the dream need only be deferred: following his presumptive reelection to the House of Representatives, La Guardia could move in earnest toward a campaign for a full four-year term as mayor, this time perhaps as the favorite. He would wait.

Meanwhile, as La Guardia sought an eighth term in Congress, he had a stronger record on which to run than ever before. The *New York Times*, at the close of 1932, looked back on the year and observed that "Throughout the session Mr. La Guardia continued to be, in many ways, the most effective leader in the House. His influence was sought; the House hung upon his words."

In March 1932 the House had passed, and later that month President Hoover had signed, the Norris–La Guardia Act. A landmark in labor relations and social legislation generally, the new statute forbade federal injunctions against the right to strike in many cases and reaffirmed labor's right to bargain collectively. It was La Guardia's signal legislative achievement, and in those years before the coming of the New Deal, an important progressive milestone.

But it turned out not to be enough to reelect its co-sponsor. Tammany selected James Lanzetta, a thirty-eight-year-old newcomer to the Board of Aldermen, to oppose their long time nemesis. Lanzetta was an engineering and law graduate of Columbia University, an East Harlem native. He worked the district hard while La Guardia remained too long in Washington. All of that would not have been enough to produce the upset. But there were two other factors.

Turnout in East Harlem in 1932 rose more than 50 percent over the 1930 midterm elections, and more than half of the additional voters came from New York's latest immigrant group, Puerto Ricans. On the way to a victory by twelve hundred votes in all, Lanzetta carried one predominantly Puerto Rican Assembly district by three thousand, probably helped along by Tammany threats to somehow identify and cut off relief benefits for anyone who voted Republican. Even larger as a contributor to Republican La Guardia's defeat was the overwhelming nature of Democrat Roosevelt's presidential victory. FDR carried La Guardia's district by twenty thousand votes.

Still, La Guardia's defeat was a shattering blow. The *Times* editorial praising his record was entitled "Exit One Gadfly," and chirped that "for two years, at least, President-elect Roosevelt will be able to keep this sand out of the party machine." La Guardia challenged the election results, complaining about having been defeated by "the importation of floaters and repeaters." When the challenge failed, he moped a bit, turning down an offer from FDR's new team to become assistant secretary of state for the administration on the grounds that he was "too old to take orders from anyone."

But by the time the 1933 campaign for mayor began, La Guardia reemerged, determined to carry the banner against Tammany at least one more time.

☐ Others, however, were not so sure. La Guardia had lost his seat, had always been somewhat unreliable politically, was more than a bit grating personally. If, as seemed certain, Mayor O'Brien would be the Tammany Democratic candidate, 1933 also appeared poised to be the year for another Fusion challenge. The issue was, who should be the challenger?

The first possibility was Joseph McKee. He had, after all, won hundreds of thousands of votes the year before without even campaigning, and O'Brien's election had automatically restored him to the post of president of the Board of Aldermen. But when his patron Flynn refused to support a Fusion candidacy, McKee resigned from office to accept a lucrative post as president of the Title Guaranty and Trust Company. He declared he was through with politics.

Through the spring and early summer of 1933, a Fusion conference committee sought a champion for their cause. La Guardia volunteered from the first, but the early consensus was that Fusion could do better. Samuel Seabury was firmly back in politics now, and a key figure in the Fusion effort. Seabury could easily have had the Fusion nomination for himself, and almost certainly could have been elected mayor, but he preferred to play kingmaker. Seabury offered to anoint Nathan Straus, Jr., but Straus also declined, feeling that with Herbert Lehman already installed as governor, and with Hitler on the rise in Germany, a Jew as mayor was not a timely notion. Literally a dozen other candidates were approached with varying degrees of seriousness, and all declined.

Finally there seemed but two alternatives to the ever-willing La Guardia. Robert Moses was the first of these. Moses had been Al Smith's New York secretary of state, and although Governor Roosevelt had declined Smith's request to reappoint him to that post, Moses remained president of the Long Island Park Commission and chairman of the New York State Parks Council. He was already something of a popular legend as the man who had, through sheer force of will, created Jones Beach and the Northern State and Southern State Parkways. In mid-July, Seabury's colleagues on the Fusion committee, frustrated, decided to nominate Moses, an enrolled Republican, and announced the fact without consulting the Judge.

Seabury, always quick to anger, was furious. He saw Moses as a creature of Smith, and Smith as a creature of Tammany. "You sold out to Tammany Hall!" he shouted at one committee member. "I'll denounce you and everybody else!" Smith, meanwhile, as if to emphasize how little Seabury understood about politics, regretfully made clear to Moses that the Happy Warrior was not (yet) prepared to bolt the Democratic party. Moses withdrew from consideration.

That left only one apparent alternative to La Guardia: John F. O'Ryan, a lawyer and retired general. Republicans within the Fusion group tried to swing the nomination to

O'Ryan, but La Guardia threatened a Republican primary, and, in any event, Seabury again intervened. O'Ryan was a protégé of Charles Whitman, the man who had defeated Seabury for governor in 1916. This made him at least as bad as Smith in Seabury's view. Scratch O'Ryan.

And so back to La Guardia. Seabury finally concurred.

Once he had the Fusion endorsement, La Guardia became the favorite, and he ran a focused campaign. First, he engineered the selection of a perfectly balanced ticket, with an Irish-American for comptroller and a Jew for president of the Board of Aldermen. While later a common political technique, at the time this was innovative—and effective. Next, whenever anyone tried to inject complex questions into the race, La Guardia insisted that "There is only one issue, and that issue is . . . Tammany Hall."

President Roosevelt wasn't happy with that focus and in particular wasn't happy with the idea that his party was about to be tossed out of New York's City Hall during his first year in the White House. Working through Flynn, Roosevelt therefore induced McKee to reenter politics, and on September 30 McKee became the candidate of the new Recovery party. Roosevelt publicly proclaimed his neutrality, but his preference was well known; McKee's campaign manager was a federal employee (on leave, of course) who owed his job to the president's patronage.

At this point the campaign seemed to spin out of control. Seabury, ever vengeful and, as always, politically tone-deaf, had taken to vicious criticism of Governor Lehman for alleged failures to crush Tammany. Lehman, in his first year as governor, was nearly as popular as FDR, and especially so with Jewish voters. Seabury's attacks on him threatened to

backfire for Fusion, and La Guardia privately begged
Seabury to stop them. But when Seabury persisted, McKee
sought to up the ante by accusing Seabury of anti-Semitism,
and publicly called on La Guardia to denounce Seabury.

For McKee this proved a fatal error. It provided an excuse
for La Guardia and his allies to circulate an article that McKee
had written in 1915, at the age of twenty-nine, for the *Catholic
World* newspaper. The article had urged Catholic parents to
support the public schools rather than surrendering them to
Jews who, McKee wrote, were somehow mixing socialism with
materialism, and religious grouping with abandonment of
their own faith. "Surely," he had told his readers, "we cannot
look for ideal results from such material."

McKee was hardly an anti-Semite; leaders of the Jewish
community from Henry Morgenthau, Sr., to Nathan Straus,
Jr., rushed to his defense. But McKee also knew that
Seabury's attacks on Lehman had not been a product of anti-
Semitism either. In any event, the incident left the McKee
campaign on the defensive and severely damaged. Roosevelt's
public declarations of neutrality came more frequently, and
may have been more heartfelt. In the end, La Guardia would
poll almost ninety thousand more Jewish votes than McKee,
with the Recovery party nominee barely edging out Tammany's O'Brien among this group.

Only one last tactic by Tammany now lay between
Fiorello La Guardia and the mayoralty: physical violence.
Election Day, November 7, 1933, was marred by more in-
timidation of voters than any such occasion in recent memory. Tammany's chief enforcer in this effort was the gangster
Dutch Schulz, who by this time had become Polly Adler's
principal customer and protector.

It was not enough. La Guardia carried every borough, winning with just over 40 percent of the vote. McKee edged O'Brien for second place overall, and in every borough except Manhattan. Four years after Jimmy Walker had crushed La Guardia, Tammany could muster less than 36 percent of the tally in Manhattan while La Guardia's combination on the Republican and Fusion lines was nearly 38 percent.

☐ It would be an overstatement to say that Fiorello La Guardia's election in 1933 marked the end of Tammany Hall. But it would be accurate to say that it marked the beginning of that end.

La Guardia served three terms as mayor, and his implacable opposition to Tammany remained a theme throughout that time. Mayor La Guardia systematically stripped the counties (boroughs) of their patronage jobs and instituted a civil service merit system.

The courts—where Tammany's problems began, where Joseph Crater achieved public office through Tammany's grace remained the last bastion of machine control. But by the end of La Guardia's mayoralty, as Warren Moscow wrote, "there was not—there could not be—a single person outside of the state and county courts who owed his job and therefore his primary allegiance to Tammany rather than to La Guardia."

In time, after that, Tammany disappeared as literally as had Joe Crater. The new Wigwam that Franklin Roosevelt had helped dedicate on the Fourth of July 1929 was the subject of foreclosure and sale by Tammany's bank. Many years later, after a second world war, Robert F. Wagner, Jr., the young man who had lived with his father the senator in an apartment in Yorkville, was elected mayor, and some talk began of the rebirth of Tammany. But in order to seek his own third term in office in 1961, Wagner had to run as an anti-Tammany candidate. He won.

EPILOGUE

☐ Popular fascination with the vanishing of Judge Crater endured even the vanishing of Tammany Hall. Twenty years after Crater was last seen, a magazine called it "the most tantalizing disappearance of our time." Ten years after that, a book called the affair "the outstanding disappearance of modern times."

Stella Crater did her best to live quietly. She spent the summer of 1931 in Belgrade Lakes, and then in 1932 took a job as a telephone operator. In 1938 she was evicted from the Fifth Avenue apartment for nonpayment of rent. Within a month she married a man named Carl Kunz in Elkton, Maryland, even though Crater, her second husband, had not yet been declared legally dead. Stella and Kunz moved to Maine full-time in 1940, spending winters in Waterville and summers in Belgrade Lakes. After twelve years of marriage (one year less than she was married to Crater), Stella and

Kunz separated, and she moved back to the New York area, taking an apartment in Brooklyn. She and Kunz were never divorced.

Stella gave occasional interviews before publishing a book on the case in 1961, called *The Empty Robe*. The *New York Times* called it "by her own admission a naive story." She moved to a nursing home in Mount Vernon, New York, in 1963, and died there in 1969.

At the close of 1938, Stella moved to have Crater's will admitted to probate, and the judge declared legally dead. She testified at the probate hearing in May 1939, saying that she now believed her former husband had died in August 1930. On June 6, 1939, the surrogate agreed, and Joseph Force Crater was declared legally dead.

A month later Stella's attorney, Emil Ellis, filed a complaint seeking the double-indemnity payments on Crater's four insurance policies that would have been due to Stella if he had been murdered. But Ellis and his client soon reached a settlement with the insurance companies under which Stella received the $30,000 face value of the policies less overdue premiums—a total of $20,561; the double-indemnity claim was dropped.

Attorney Ellis also advanced a new theory of Crater's disappearance and secured the enthusiastic cooperation of the *New York Mirror* in advancing it. The theory centered on yet another showgirl, this one named June Brice. Brice, Ellis and the *Mirror* said, had herself disappeared in September 1930 after attempting to extort money from Crater. (This account left vague whether Brice was the same person as Samuel Buchler's "Lorraine Fay.") Thereafter, the story continued, mobster friends of Brice had abducted and killed Crater.

The *Mirror* duly located Brice, but she was confined to Pilgrim State Hospital in Brentwood, New York, on Long Island, and was suffering from both tuberculosis and dementia. She could not confirm—or deny—the tale; her mother said June had known Judge Crater but had always refused to discuss the Crater case. Of course, another showgirl knowing Crater should not have surprised anyone by then.

This wasn't much on which to base a theory, and the fact that Brice's name had not appeared at all in any of the major newspapers in 1930, when so many other women's names had, seemed to undercut it further. (Ellis may have confused Brice with Jane Manners, a woman whose name had surfaced momentarily in mid-September 1930 as one of Crater's many lady friends.) Certainly the insurance companies didn't find the Brice theory persuasive. But Stella told interviewers beginning in the 1950s that she believed her husband had been murdered, and in her 1961 book she seemed to endorse Ellis's Brice theory. It still reappears in many brief accounts of the case today. It shouldn't.

Other theories continued to abound. One account placed Judge Crater alive and well and living in Africa. Yet another tried to revive the Vivian Gordon link. A 1959 article in *Harper's* related that a psychic had identified the location of Crater's body, in the yard of a house in Yonkers, New York. The Westchester County sheriff had the yard dug up, in part for the benefit of cameras from *Life* magazine, but nothing was found.

Polly Adler died in 1962 without ever discussing Judge Crater's fate publicly—or responding to the suggestion that she knew all about it. In 1964 *A House Is Not a Home* was made into a very forgettable movie starring Shelley Winters.

The Missing Persons Bureau of the New York Police Department continued to carry the disappearance of Joseph Crater as an open file until August 13, 1979—almost fifty years. By the time the case was closed, Crater would have been ninety years old.

In 1971 the NYPD began one of its periodic efforts to update the file. In doing so, the Missing Persons Bureau sought help first in locating the citizen who had filed their initial report. Where, they inquired of the Association of the Bar, was someone named Simon Rifkind?

Rifkind claimed to be "amused" but clearly was not. He had been appointed a federal district judge by FDR in 1941, at the instance of Senator Wagner, and had served nine years on the federal bench. Since 1950 he had been a name partner in the law firm Paul, Weiss, Rifkind, Wharton and Garrison, and an occasional adviser to Presidents Eisenhower, Kennedy, and Johnson. He had even briefly been third deputy commissioner of the NYPD. He should not have been hard to find.

Rifkind alerted the *New York Times* to the inquiry and told the *Times* reporter, "If they can't find me, how could they ever find Crater?"

But he also declined to answer Chief Inspector Michael Codd's letter. "Besides, he said, the letter only deepened the mystery and he had nothing to add to the files."

Some years later, interviewed again on the Crater case, this time by *New York* magazine, Rifkind went a bit further. His part in the Crater case, he said, had been "peripheral." His submission of the original missing person's report was merely a "technicality."

ACKNOWLEDGMENTS

☐ I write books for the pleasure of doing so—and (I hope) for the pleasure they may bring to readers. One of the reasons writing has proven such a pleasure for me is the willingness of countless people to help.

For assistance in assembling research materials, I owe thanks to Diane Windham Shaw of the Lafayette College library; Raymond Teichman of the Franklin D. Roosevelt Presidential Library, Bill Pollak, Kris Fischer, and Jean Conway of American Lawyer Media, publishers of the *New York Law Journal*; Deborah Panella of the Paul Weiss law firm; and Sally Locke of the Columbia University library. Ed Adler at Time Warner and his colleague Stacey Hoppe at Warner Bros. took the time to check an obscure fact. Some research efforts inevitably yield "dry holes," but these also require assistance in the drilling, so thanks also to the

Hon. Albert Rosenblatt of the New York Court of Appeals; Jennifer Gilmore of Harcourt publishers; Thomas Mooney of the University of Nebraska–Lincoln library; Luis Mocete of the Proskauer Rose law firm; and Ralph Monaco of the New York County Lawyers Association.

For pointing me in fruitful directions and encouraging my work I thank my friends David Glasser, Jody Adams, and Jed Bernstein, and Jed's friend Billy Sternberg. For offering help in finding this book a publishing home I thank Allen Barra, Kevin Baker, and Sam Roberts.

Peter Tucker and Mitch Portnoy provided invaluable research assistance, and I am indebted as well to the staffs of the New York Public Library and the Rare Books and Manuscripts Library at Columbia University. My friend Arthur Sulzberger and his colleagues Jim Mones, Dennis Laurie, and Louis Ferrer of the *New York Times* helped me locate photos.

My friends Lou Grumet, David Glasser, and Gordon Crovitz took time to read the manuscript and made a number of valuable suggestions. Readers Hon. Leonard Sand and Peter Quinn also lent much-appreciated support. Ivan Dee's editing significantly improved the book and well served both reader and author. Needless to say, the errors these people didn't catch were my fault, and still are.

This book is dedicated to my parents. My father, Robert L. Tofel, taught me from a very early age about the nobility of the law, a lesson that seems to have eluded Joseph Crater. My late mother, Carol Collins Tofel, long ago gave me the confidence to think I could do things like writing books while working full-time. Part of the germ for this book, more than thirty years ago, was reading my father's copy of Herbert Mitgang's *The Man Who Rode the Tiger* and hearing my mother's tales of the adventures of Philip Haberman, a dear friend of my maternal grandparents and one of Judge Seabury's "boys."

My wife, Jeanne Straus, is also my best friend and my first editor. She didn't just improve this book, she made it possible, as she does so much of my life. (Her paternal grandfather also makes a cameo appearance toward the end of the story.) Our daughter, Rachel Straus Tofel, suggested the title, and even claimed to enjoy the manuscript. Our son, Colin Straus Tofel, continued to make me laugh more easily and deeply than anyone else ever has. No husband, father, or author could ask for more.

R. J. T.

Riverdale, New York
May 2004

SOURCES

☐ I reviewed all of the 1930–1931 coverage of the Crater case in four of New York's daily newspapers: the *Times*, the *Herald Tribune*, the *Sun*, and the *World*, as well as a good bit of that in the *Daily News* and the legal newspaper the *New York Law Journal*. This was supplemented by various later newspaper articles and by assorted clippings found in the scrapbooks of the Kilroe Collection of Tammaniana in the Rare Book and Manuscript Library at Columbia University and in the archives of Lafayette College, Joseph Crater's alma mater. Specific references to these sources can be found in the notes. Beyond them, I found the following sources to be most helpful:

Adler, Polly, *A House Is Not a Home* (New York, Rinehart & Co., 1953).

Alexander, Jack, "What Happened to Judge Crater?," *Saturday Evening Post*, September 10, 1960.

Asbury, Herbert, *The Gangs of New York: An Informal History of the Underworld* (New York, Alfred A. Knopf, 1928; Thunder's Mouth Press paperback, 2002).

Sources

Ayers, John, and Carol Bird, *Missing Men: The Story of the Missing Persons Bureau of the New York Police Department* (New York, G. P. Putnam's Sons, 1932).

Bellush, Bernard, *Franklin D. Roosevelt as Governor of New York* (New York, Columbia University Press, 1955).

Black, Conrad, *Franklin Delano Roosevelt: Champion of Freedom* (New York, Public Affairs Press, 2003).

Bloom, Murray Teigh, "Is It Judge Crater's Body?" *Harper's*, November 1959.

Brodsky, Alyn, *The Great Mayor: Fiorello La Guardia and the Making of the City of New York* (New York, St. Martin's Press, 2003).

Brooks, John, "Advocate," *New Yorker*, May 23, 1983.

Brooks, John, *Once in Golconda: A True Drama of Wall Street, 1920–1938* (New York, Harper & Row, 1969).

Bryce, James, *The American Commonwealth*, 2 vols. (New York, Macmillan, 1891).

Caro, Robert, *The Power Broker: Robert Moses and the Fall of New York* (New York, Alfred A. Knopf, 1974; Vintage paperback, 1975).

Chambers, Walter, *Samuel Seabury: A Challenge* (New York, The Century Co., 1932).

Churchill, Allen, *They Never Came Back* (New York, Ace Books, 1960).

Connable, Alfred, and Edward Silberfarb, *Tigers of Tammany: Nine Men Who Ran New York* (New York, Holt, Rinehart and Winston, 1967).

Crater, Stella, with Oscar Frawley, *The Empty Robe: The Story of the Disappearance of Judge Crater* (New York, Doubleday, 1961).

Davis, Kenneth, *FDR: The New York Years, 1928–1933* (New York, Random House, 1994).

Ellis, Edward Robb, *The Epic of New York City* (New York, Coward-McCann, 1966).

Finan, Christopher, *Alfred E. Smith: The Happy Warrior* (New York, Hill and Wang, 2002).

Finegan, James, *Tammany at Bay* (New York, Dodd, Mead, 1933).

Flynn, Edward, *You're the Boss* (New York, Viking, 1947).

Fowler, Gene, *Beau James: The Life and Times of Jimmy Walker* (New York, Viking, 1949).

Friedel, Frank, *Franklin D. Roosevelt: The Apprenticeship* (Boston, Little, Brown, 1952).

Gannett, Robert, "Good Night, Judge Crater, Wherever You Are . . .," *New York* magazine, August 11, 1980.

Gribetz, Louis, and Joseph Kaye, *Jimmie Walker: The Story of a Personality* (New York, Dial Press, 1932).

Handlin, Oscar, *Al Smith and His America* (Boston, Atlantic Monthly Press/Little Brown, 1958).

Huthmacher, J. Joseph, *Senator Robert Wagner and the Rise of Urban Liberalism* (New York, Atheneum, 1968).

Jeffers, H. Paul, *The Napoleon of New York: Mayor Fiorello La Guardia* (New York, John Wiley & Sons, 2002).

Johnson, Alva, "The Scandals of New York," *Harper's*, March 1931.

Kessner, Thomas, *Fiorello H. La Guardia and the Making of Modern New York* (New York, McGraw-Hill, 1989).

LaCerra, Charles, *Franklin Delano Roosevelt and Tammany Hall of New York* (Lanham, Md., University Press of America, 1997).

Lindley, Ernest K., *Franklin D. Roosevelt: A Career in Progressive Democracy* (Indianapolis, Bobbs-Merrill, 1931).

Lowi, Theodore, *At the Pleasure of the Mayor: Patronage and Power in New York City, 1898–1958* (Glencoe, Ill., Free Press, 1964).

Mackaye, Milton, *The Tin Box Parade. A Handbook for Tammany* (New York, Robert M. McBride & Co., 1934).

Mann, Arthur, *La Guardia Comes to Power, 1933* (Chicago, University of Chicago Press, 1965; Phoenix paperback, 1969).

Manning, Gordon, "The Most Tantalizing Disappearance of Our Time," *Collier's*, July 29, 1950.

Mitgang, Herbert, *Once Upon a Time in New York: Jimmy Walker, Franklin Roosevelt, and the Last Great Battle of the Jazz Age* (New York, Free Press, 2000).

Mitgang, Herbert, *The Man Who Rode the Tiger: The Life and Times of Judge Samuel Seabury* (Philadelphia, Lippincott, 1963; Fordham University Press ed., 1996).

Moley, Raymond, *27 Masters of Politics: In a Personal Perspective* (New York, Funk & Wagnalls, 1949).

Moley, Raymond, *Tribunes of the People: The Past and Future of the New York Magistrates' Courts* (New Haven, Yale University Press, 1932).

Moscow, Warren, *Politics in the Empire State* (New York, Alfred A. Knopf, 1948).

Mushkat, Jerome, *Tammany: The Evolution of a Political Machine, 1789–1865* (Syracuse, Syracuse University Press, 1971).

Nash, Jay Robert, *Among the Missing: An Anecdotal History of Missing Persons from 1800 to the Present* (New York, Simon & Schuster, 1978).

Nevins, Allan, *Herbert H. Lehman and His Era* (New York, Scribner's, 1963).

Northrop, William, and John Northrop, *The Insolence of Office: The Story of the Seabury Investigations* (New York, G. P. Putnam's Sons, 1932).

Pietrusza, David, *Rothstein: The Life, Times, and Murder of the Criminal Genius Who Fixed the 1919 World Series* (New York, Carroll & Graf, 2003).

Pringle, Henry, *Alfred E. Smith: A Critical Study* (New York, Macy, Masius, 1927).

Pringle, Henry, "Profiles: The Janitor's Boy," *New Yorker*, March 5, 1927.

Pringle, Henry, "Tammany Hall, Inc.," *Atlantic Monthly*, October 1932.

Proskauer, Joseph, *A Segment of My Times* (New York, Farrar, Straus, 1950).

Rifkind, Simon, *One Man's Word: Selected Works of Simon H. Rifkind*, 3 vols. (privately printed, 1986, 1989).

Sloat, Warren, *A Battle for the Soul of New York: Tammany Hall, Police Corruption, Vice, and Reverend Charles Parkhurst's Crusade Against Them, 1892–1895* (New York, Cooper Square Press, 2002).

Smith, Alfred E., *Up to Now: An Autobiography* (New York, Viking, 1929).

Stewart, Gail, *What Happened to Judge Crater* (New York, Crestwood House, 1992).

von Drehle, David, *Triangle: The Fire That Changed America* (New York, Atlantic Monthly Press, 2003).

Walker, Stanley, *City Editor* (New York, Frederick A. Stokes Co., 1934; Johns Hopkins University Press paperback, 1999).

Walker, Stanley, *Mrs. Astor's Horse* (New York, Frederick A. Stokes Co., 1935).

Walsh, George, *Gentleman Jimmy Walker: Mayor of the Jazz Age* (New York, Praeger, 1974).

"Weird Clue in the Crater Mystery," *Life*, November 16, 1959.

Weiss, Nancy, *Charles Francis Murphy, 1858–1924: Respectability and Responsibility in Tammany Politics* (Northampton, Mass., Smith College, 1968).

Werner, M. R., *Tammany Hall* (New York, Doubleday, Doran, 1928).

Whelan, Frank, "The Mystery of Judge Crater," *Allentown Morning-Call*, January 15, 1989.

NOTES

☐   References to authors, unless otherwise indicated, are to their books and articles listed under Sources.

ABBREVIATIONS:
NYDN, New York Daily News
NYHT, New York Herald Tribune
NYLJ, New York Law Journal
NYT, New York Times
Sun, New York Sun
World, New York World

Page

16   Crater was replaced by Rifkind. Rifkind's accounts of his long and distinguished career later omitted Crater's role in his securing the job with Wagner, and suggested his service had begun later in 1926, only after Wagner was elected to the U.S. Senate, rather than when he ascended to the Appellate Division.

17   "Our chat was quite good-humored and informal": Manning, p. 64.

17   Crater did not know how to drive: Ayers, p. 220.

18   "somewhat mutilated": NYPD Missing Persons circular for Crater, September 8, 1930.

Notes

18 Elaine Dawn later testified that Crater was accompanied by Klein; *NYT* of October 3, 1930, and *World* of October 8, 1930, say it was Kaplan. It is possible both were correct.

19 "a night club of sordid reputation": Crater, p. 99.

19 "white light rendezvous": *World*, September 10, 1930.

19 Club Abbey owned by "Owney" Madden: Churchill, p. 74.

19 "Owney the Killer": Asbury, p. 322.

19 "a few judicious armed robberies": Walsh, pp. 144–145.

20 "He did not toss in many chips": *NYHT*, September 10, 1930.

22 Rising of the Empire State Building: Ric Burns and James Sanders, *New York: An Illustrated History* (New York, Alfred A. Knopf, 1999), p. 379.

22 The *Daily News*'s new tower: Walker, *City Editor*, p. 67.

22 Votes for repeal in New York: Walsh, p. 97.

23 Roosevelt had been sailing with Black in 1921: Lindley, pp. 200–201.

24 Median family spending in New York: Mann, p. 125.

26 Religious breakdown of New York population: Mann, p. 125.

27 Overturning forty-nine prior rulings: Bellush, p. 307, n.12.

27 "a broker in political chicanery": Mackaye, p. 60.

29 Not a strong swimmer: *NYHT*, September 10, 1930.

30 "something like a turtle walking upright": Churchill, p. 60.

30 "glib brittle, machine-made romances": *World*, August 6, 1930.

30 Saw a preview in Atlantic City: Alexander, p. 20.

30 Recollection of the Arrow clerk: *World*, September 3, 1960; *Sun*, September 13, 1960.

31 Talked with Bowers: *Sun*, September 12, 1960.

31 The ticket was later picked up. Detective Hugh Sheridan of the New York Police Department later stated with apparent certainty that Crater did not attend that evening's performance, but the basis of this claim was not stated and is not known. *Sun*, September 13, 1930.

31 Crater's dinner: Billy Haas, quoted in *Sun*, September 24, 1960.

31 Perhaps Crater was unconcerned. Ritz also later recalled that Crater had said he was going for a swim and then back to Maine the next morning, but her testimony to this effect came only after Mara's account had been published, and thus may not deserve much weight on this point.

34 The nomenclature of Tammany: Mann, p. 48; Mitgang, *Once Upon a Time*, p. 41.

34 "sanguine enough to hope everything": Werner, pp. 19–20.

34 Davis convicted of fraud: Mitgang, *Once Upon a Time*, p. 41.

35 Wood's margin of victory: Brodsky, p. 31.

35 Wood's refusal to enforce Sunday closings: Asbury, p. 96.

35 Wood advocates a free state: Connable and Silberfarb, p. 134.

36 "Statesman!": Mitgang, *Once Upon a Time*, p. 43.

36 "a large, pleasure-loving population": Werner, p. 406.

37 "When you've voted 'em . . .": Werner, p. 439. Sullivan is little remembered today, though his "Sullivan Law," banning concealed handguns from New York, remains on the books. Walsh, p. 25.

37 "These reform movements are like queen hornets": Werner, p. 444.

38 "they lived from 'reform' to 'reform' ": Flynn, p. 8.

39 Murphy left no letters: Weiss, p. 3.

39 "Most of the troubles of the world": Mitgang, *Once Upon a Time*, p. 44.

39 Increases in Murphy's wealth: See Weiss, p. 23.

39 Wagner dismissed charges against Murphy: Weiss, p. 63.

40 "Well young lady . . .": Weiss, p. 88.

40 "a sense of proportion": Johnson, p. 41.

40 "the cradle of modern liberalism": Huthmacher, pp. 35–36.

40 "The brains went out of Tammany Hall": Huthmacher, p. 37.

41 Twenty-three districts with thirty-five leaders: *NYT*, October 5, 1930, section 10.

41 District leaders holding public jobs: *NYT*, September 29, 1930.

42 "the best representative of the worst element": Walsh, p. 221.

42 Smith family birthplaces: Smith, p. 85.

42 Smith was younger when he left school: Black, p. 122.

42 "I had a choice of hard labor . . .": Finan, p. 35.

42 Smith was a stranger to Albany: Smith, p. 69.

42 "I was diligent in my attendance": Smith, p. 71.

43 "I had never been in a bank": Caro, p. 160.

44 "His taste for good clothes": Huthmacher, p. 18.

44 Wagner "was not an introspective man": Huthmacher, p. 33.

45 "I mean Bob Wagner": Huthmacher, p. 41.

45 Wagner's religion disqualified him: Huthmacher, p. 50. Wagner converted to Catholicism in 1946: Huthmacher, p. 340.

45 "the most glorious moment of my life": Huthmacher, p. 51.

46 Smith's salary as sheriff: Smith, p. 152.

46 Smith used his influence: Pringle, *Alfred E. Smith*, p. 148.

46 He began an extension on his home: Smith, p. 152.

46 "up from the city streets": Handlin, p. 67.

47 "The raucous voice and the brown derby": Proskauer, p. 49.

Notes

47 "I'm supposed to know Benjamin Franklin": Proskauer, p. 46.

47 FDR deferred to Smith: See Lindley, p. 165.

47 "the most thorough renovation of a state government": Moscow, p. 11.

48 The evening was a triumph for Smith: Finan, pp. 135–138.

48 "I am called upon to wage the real fight": Walsh, p. 94.

48 "an extraordinary personal and political triumph": Quoted in Finan, p. 156.

49 "the delegates wrestled . . . with their ambitions": Walsh, p. 11.

49 "the new Smith emerged": Pringle, *Alfred E. Smith*, pp. 58–59.

50 "I am the leader of the Democracy in New York": Pringle, *Alfred E. Smith*, p. 18.

50 "the most powerful leader": Quoted in Finan, p. 191.

51 Gifts from Chadbourne: Finan, p. 160.

51 Fewer people used his first name to his face: Pringle, *Alfred E. Smith*, pp. 278–279.

51 Smith signed the repeal: See Flynn, pp. 40–41.

51 "the time hasn't come when a man can say his beads": Finan, p. 230.

51 Five times what he had received as governor: Caro, p. 293.

52 Gift from Raskob: Finan, pp. 234–235.

52 "It is a fiction . . .": Mackaye, p. 29.

52 "the most charming Mayor": Pringle, *Alfred E. Smith*, p. 128.

52 "New York wore James J. Walker in its lapel": Ellis, p. 526.

53 "both the demolition and reconstruction crews": *NYT*, July 9, 1930.

53 The objects of politics were entirely local: Gribetz and Kaye, pp. 13–15.

54 His political career was at an end: Fowler, pp. 48–49; Werner, p. 512; Walsh, p. 21.

55 "and he rides twice as fast": Mitgang, *Once Upon a Time*, p. 67.

55 Walker took the rostrum: Gribetz and Kaye, pp. 81–82.

56 "Is the bill still at the desk?": Gribetz and Kaye, pp. 85–86.

56 "Why all this talk about womanhood?": Fowler, p. 106.

56 With a strong assist from Flynn: Flynn, pp. 51, 54.

56 "I've not read more than fifteen books": Fowler, p. 34.

57 "Did you say Citizen Union?": Kessner, p. 158.

57 Bored after six weeks: Fowler, p. 174.

57 Walker's travels: Fowler, p. 219; see also Walsh, pp. 160–161.

57 Smith had never left the country: Pringle, *Alfred E. Smith*, p. 84.

57 "gorgeous dressing gowns and pajamas": Gribetz and Kaye, pp. 277–278.

58 "the waist-line must be just so": Gribetz and Kaye, p. 279.

58 "three shades of the same solid color": Gribetz and Kaye, p. 278.

58 "a man's beard is his own fault": Kessner, p. 158.

58 Walker "couldn't stand being mauled": Fowler, p. 86.

59 Seemingly without a care: Fowler, pp. 86–87.

59 Two hours late for the wedding: Mitgang, *Once Upon a Time*, p. 66.

59 "We were always happy together": Fowler, p. 111.

59 "Use your own judgment": Walsh, p. 34.

60 Talk of Walker for governor: Fowler, p. 110.

60 Walker broke off the relationship: Fowler, pp. 142–145.

60 Code-named "Boy Friend": Walsh, p. 147.

60 Compton's background: Walsh, p. 169.

61 Walker's salary raised: Ellis, p. 526.

61 Just weeks inside the legal deadline: Finegan, p. 122.

61 Allie Walker's clothes charges: Walker, *Mrs. Astor's Horse*, p. 177.

61 Summoned to the cardinal's residence: Kessner, p. 200.

61 "The Mayor He Might Be": *NYT*, July 20, 1929.

63 "a balanced ticket all by himself": Mann, p. 26.

63 La Guardia's Americanization: Jeffers, pp. 10, 16.

63 "Free masonry is my religion": Jeffers, p. 114.

63 Calling himself "Frank": Kessner, p. 27.

63 A pension of eight dollars per month: Kessner, p. 17.

63 His health would never fully recover: Kessner, p. 18.

64 Earning $1,200 per year: Kessner, p. 24.

65 La Guardia stuck with the Republicans: Kessner, pp. 32–33.

65 "he was listed as 'Floullo'": Kessner, pp. 33–34.

65 "sounded like an older choir boy's tenor-alto": Mann, p. 17.

65 La Guardia threatened a primary: Kessner, p. 38.

65 First Italian-American in Congress: Kessner, p. 43.

66 "pure hands and glands": Kessner, p. 54.

67 "a Jew with a Jewish heart": Kessner, p. 92.

67 *"ENTIRELY IN THE YIDDISH LANGUAGE"*: Jeffers, pp. 104–105; Kessner, p. 92; capitals and italics in original.

67 A margin of eleven votes: Jeffers, p. 108.

68 "the Socialist Party doesn't pretend": Brodsky, p. 109.

68 "the Belasco of politics": Kessner, p. 112.

68 La Guardia's coverage in *NYT*: Jeffers, p. 123.

68 He called another press conference: Kessner, pp. 112–113.

69 La Guardia's courage: Kessner, p. 132; Brodsky, p. 208.

70 "We must fight fire with fire": Kessner, p. 143.

70 "first and foremost, a professional pol": Brodsky, p. 54.

Notes

70 "And he's proud he's a Wop": Kessner, p. 161.

70 "Elect a full time Mayor": Kessner, p. 161.

71 "a man can wear his own clothes": Moley, 27 *Masters of Politics*, p. 207.

71 "cheap gamblers . . . used my name": Walsh, p. 173.

72 "The political geniuses of Tammany": Asbury, p. 34.

72 "all manner of services": Walsh, p. 172.

72 "there are now no gangs in New York": Asbury, p. xiv.

73 Three-day gambling marathon: Pietrusza, pp. 8, 12, 355.

73 "Won't talk about it": Mitgang, *Once Upon a Time*, p. 12.

74 McManus was acquitted: Pietrusza, pp. 311–314.

74 The "Al Capone of New York": *NYHT*, October 19, 1930.

75 "It would have meant a slaughter": Walsh, p. 206.

75 The robbers' take: Mitgang, *Once Upon a Time*, p. 98; Pietrusza, pp. 332–333.

75 " 'There is your gun' ": Walsh, p. 206.

76 The police tried to blame Terranova: Pietrusza, pp. 333–334.

76 "they make a goat out of me": *NYHT*, October 19, 1930.

76 Vitale's loan arrangements: Walsh, pp. 200–201.

76 Vitale released a friend of Rothstein: Pietrusza, pp. 334–335.

76 Vitale removed from office: *NYLJ*, March 14, 1930.

76 " 'I told you so' ": *NYHT*, October 19, 1930.

77 Only the second Democrat from his district: Friedel, p. 89.

78 "The lawmaker behind desk 26": *NYT*, January 22, 1911, quoted in Lindley, p. 88.

79 "a monstrous travesty of politics": Quoted in Finan, p. 77.

80 "the most humanly interesting political fight in many years": Quoted in Finan, p. 77.

80 Smith and Wagner at the Roosevelts: Finan, p. 72.

80 Roosevelt and Murphy meet: Lindley, p. 92.

82 "One year in Albany": Lindley, p. 100.

82 "Beloved and Revered Future President": Davis, p. 9.

83 "The attempted Clark stampede disintegrated": Lindley, p. 104.

84 "blood is thicker than water": Lindley, p. 131.

84 " 'Get up, New York!' ": Lindley, p. 190.

85 Cox consulted with Murphy: Handlin, p. 115.

85 "a genius who kept harmony": LaCerra, p. 61.

85 Roosevelt and Tammany's new headquarters: Bellush, pp. 154, 212, 307, n.6.

86 "it must have the approval of Tammany": *NYT*, March 22, 1930.

87 Roosevelt was in a bind: See *Sun*, September 6, 1930.

88 "I found that was a great protection": Robert Jackson, *That Man: An Insider's Portrait of Franklin D. Roosevelt* (New York, Oxford University Press, 2003), p. 56.

90 Crater active in professional societies: *NYLJ*, April 10, 1930.

90 Members of the Special Calendar Committee: *NYT*, October 9, 1930.

91 "a lawyer of capacity and distinct ability": *NYLJ*, April 10, 1930.

91 FDR "has acted wisely and with sound judgment": *NYLJ*, April 12, 1930.

92 "well qualified to be on the bench": *NYT*, April 10, 1930.

94 "I was not overly concerned": Crater, p. 81.

94 "he had seen him around": Crater, p. 159. Mrs. Crater's book, which was written more than twenty years after her testimony, and which notes that Rifkind later became a federal judge, says that Rifkind was "surprised" that Crater was not in Belgrade Lakes.

95 Rifkind's and Quillinan's inquiries: *World*, September 23, 1930.

95 Kahler's trip to New York: *NYHT*, September 23, 1930. Alexander, p. 45, says Kahler was dispatched on August 11 and hired a private detective August 15, but no source is given, and this seems not to account for Rifkind's earlier role.

95 "P.S. . . . I do need some money": *World*, October 8, 1930. Remarkably, Mrs. Crater does not mention this letter, or the wire to which it replied, in her book. On the other hand, Rifkind does not appear to have challenged this published account at the time.

95 "It looks as if everything is all right": Crater, p. 84.

96 Stella was nearly incoherent: Crater, p. 84.

96 "for personal reasons": *NYT*, September 5, 1930.

97 Purchasing *The Just Lawyer*: Fowler, pp. 274–275; Mann, p. 46.

98 " a disgrace for Supreme Court justices": Chambers, p. 68.

99 Supported Hearst for governor: Chambers, pp. 100–108.

100 "Mr. President, you are a blatherskite!": Mann, p. 46.

100 "an aloof, superior air": Mitgang, *Once Upon a Time*, p. 100.

100 "he could invest the blowing of his nose with theological overtones": Walsh, p. 223.

100 No one called him "Sam": Mackaye, p. 298.

101 "I find it impossible to raise you to the level of my contempt": Chambers, p. 92.

101 "*you* were never worth that much to anybody": Mitgang, *The Man Who Rode the Tiger*, p. 221; emphasis in original.

Notes

101 "telephoning everyone of whom I could think": Crater, p. 86.

102 "She was hysterical": *NYHT*, September 5, 1930.

102 What was *not* missing: Crater, p. 88.

102 "I don't think anything should be done until he gets here": Crater, p. 88.

104 "a voting residence": *NYHT*, September 4, 1930.

104 a "political nest": *Sun*, September 5, 1930.

104 Telegram to Roosevelt: *New York American* to FDR, 3:10 P.M., September 3, 1930, in FDR Library files.

104 Rifkind's interview with the *New Yorker*: reproduced in Rifkind, vol. I, p. 38.

105 Rifkind's omissions were intentional: See *Sun*, September 5, 1930.

105 "He was extremely careful of his conduct": *Sun*, September 5, 1930.

106 "a very competent man": *NYHT*, September 5, 1930.

107 "It has generally been believed until yesterday . . .": *NYT*, September 5, 1930.

107 "whacking a golf ball": Huthmacher, p. 121.

107 A curious approach for friends: *NYHT*, September 5, 1930.

108 Crater's tattoo: Contemporary accounts differ on whether the tattoo was on the left arm or the right; Mrs. Crater's book does not say.

109 "a very short time when one stops to think": *World*, September 10, 1930.

109 Elaine Dawn's illness: *Sun*, September 9, 1930; *NYHT*, September 10, 1930.

109 "they all liked him": *Sun*, September 9, 1930.

110 "And not friends in the Broadway sense, either": *NYDN*, September 10, 1930.

110 Jane Manners and Emmita Casanova: *NYT*, September 12, 1930; *Sun*, September, 12, 1930.

110 Marie Miller and Crater: *NYT*, September 14, 1930; *Sun*, September 18, 1930.

111 Preview of "Dancing Partner": *NYT*, September 8, 12, 1930; Alexander, p. 20.

111 The *World* suggested an inquiry: *World*, September 10, 1930.

111 "the obvious method of procedure": *World*, September 11, 1930.

111 Lippmann's editorials: *World*, September 10–13, 1930.

112 "an ineffectual but honest man": Fowler, p. 299.

112 Crain's early career: von Drehle, p. 256.

113 Crain was miscast: Mackaye, p. 31.

115 Stella at secretarial school: Crater, p. 14.

115 Stella's work in New York: Crater, p. 16.
115 "to whom I suddenly found myself married": Crater, pp. 26–27.
116 "from that day forward": Crater, p. 18.
116 Stella's answers to Crain's questions: The full text of Mrs. Crater's replies, and Crain's questions, was published in the *Sun* of September 17, 1930 and the *NYT*, *NYHT*, and *World* of September 18, 1930.
117 "I am going to have her here": *NYHT*, September 18, 1930.
118 "The sky spun and I feel on my knees": Crater, p. 104.
119 Letter to the *World*: The text of the letter appeared in the *World* on September 18, 1930.
120 Buchler's description of "Fay" to the *World*: *World*, September 18, 1930.
121 Buchler's description of "Fay" to the *Sun*: *Sun*, September 18, 1930.
122 "cloak model and saleswoman": Crater, p. 100.
122 " 'Joe and I were ideally happy' ": Ayers, pp. 5, 6.
123 Description of Marcus: Churchill, pp. 73–74.
123 Crater's payments to Marcus: Alexander, p. 44.
123 Crater and Marcus's last evening together: *NYHT*, September 27, 1930; *World*, September 27, 1930.
123 An attempt to distract the public?: *Sun*, September 20, 1930.
125 "the month apple-sellers became prevalent": Brooks, *Once in Golconda*, p. 130.
127 In full judicial regalia: Chambers, p. 228.
128 Mistaken notice in the *Law Journal*: *World*, October 5, 1930.
128 Crain did not ask Healy or Ewald: *Sun*, October 4, 1930.
130 Crater's stock sales through McCabe: Crater had also purchased some of the shares he now sold through Reinhardt & Bennett, but it is not clear if that account was still open in May 1930.
130 FDR had been an original backer of International Germanic Trust: Black, p. 151.
130 "Joe Crater was in the know": *NYT*, October 6, 1930.
131 Lippmann took up the cry: *World*, October 8, 1930.
132 "living such a wretched loose life": *NYT*, October 9, 1930.
134 "I would be the last one to help them assassinate his character": Crater, p. 112.
136 "I speak for the heart and conscience": Bellush, p. 160.
136 "That is American. That is right": Davis, p. 188.
137 "Healy is said to be only leader in name": *NYHT*, October 19, 1930.
137 Roosevelt's vote in 1930: Bellush, pp. 172–173.
139 "I felt I could go home": Crater, p. 124.

Notes

140 The drawer where the envelopes were found: *NYT*, May 12, 1939.
140 The cash withdrawn on August 6: *World*, January 23, 1931.
142 The failure of the Libby Hotel: *NYDN*, September 20, 1930.
143 Levy's later recollection: *World*, January 25, 1931.
144 Stella recalled discussing the Libby: Crater, p. 72.
145 "as soon as I recovered from my shock": Crater, pp. 168, 130.
149 Stella received less than $11,000: Manning, p. 64.
150 "not due to any lack of personal effort": Mitgang, *Once Upon a Time*, pp. 130–131.
151 "it was all due to politics": Crater, p. 206.
153 Adler's customers: Adler, *passim*; Pietrusza, p. 350.
154 Berger review of *A House Is Not a Home*: *NYT*, June 14, 1953.
154 "a full cement-coffin burial": Churchill, p. 80.
155 Adler insists she did not meet Schulz until later: Adler, pp. 201–206.
155 "apparently overmastered": Adler, p. 167.
159 Acuna at the Seabury hearings: Chambers, pp. 242–243.
160 Magistrate Norris's corruption: Northrop and Northrop, p. 90.
160 Crater's ostensible visit to Sing Sing: Churchill, pp. 81–82; Crater, pp. 145–147.
161 Links to Vivian Gordon: Churchill, pp. 83–84; *NYDN*, February 28, 1999.
161 "Are you going to tell me with whom you split your fees?": Chambers, p. 305.
161 "a crucification": Mitgang, *Once Upon a Time*, p. 136.
161 Comparisons of salary and income: Mann, pp. 53–54.
162 "It was in a tin box": Mackaye, p. 306.
162 Farley's career: Mackaye, p. 189.
163 "It was a wonderful box": Mackaye, pp. 195–196.
163 FDR, working with Moley: Moley, *27 Masters of Politics*, p. 214.
164 "when a public official in under inquiry or investigation": *NYT*, February 18, 1932.
165 "Round One Won by Walker": *Literary Digest*, May 9, 1931.
166 "would serve their God as they seek to serve themselves": Bellush, p. 280.
166 "Little Boy Blue is about to blow his horn": Mitgang, *Once Upon a Time*, pp. 143–144.
166 "I'd be most happy to give you *my* seat": Fowler, pp. 302–303.
167 "'How much salary does the Mayor get'": Mackaye, p. 268.
167 "available for Mrs. Walker and myself": Walsh, p. 306.

167 Bus franchise award: Bellush, p. 274.

167 Letter of credit delivered to Walker: Walsh, p. 121.

167 Made good on a Walker overdraft: Bellush, p. 275.

168 Walker claimed he had been at risk of loss: Walsh, p. 208; Fowler, p. 311; Bellush, p. 275.

168 Taking them in a car would have been unseemly: Fowler, pp. 311–312.

168 Joint checking and brokerage accounts: Walsh, p. 280.

168 Referred to as the "unnamed person": Fowler, p. 311.

168 Some of the money appeared to come from Block: Mackaye, p. 316.

168 Kickbacks on city contracts: Walsh, p. 280.

168 Fee-splitting by doctors: Bellush, p. 274.

169 Sherwood and Seabury's subpoena: Walsh, pp. 280–281.

169 "left the witness stand trailing clouds": Quoted in Walsh, p. 315.

169 "a failure so deep as to make one's flesh creep": Quoted in Bellush, p. 276.

170 "he would have been a far bigger man": *World*, November 3, 1930.

171 "a menace to the nation as well": *Literary Digest*, March 12, 1932.

172 "Good old Jimsie!": Fowler, p. 316.

173 "So you'd rather be right than President!": Moley, *27 Masters of Politics*, p. 211.

173 "he has been studiously unfair": *NYT*, September 2, 1932.

174 "submitting my case to the people who made me Mayor": *NYT*, September 2, 1932.

174 McKee and *The Captive*: Mackaye, pp. 258–259.

175 "Walker slighted his job, and McKee worked at his": Mackaye, p. 258.

175 He retained a limousine for himself: Mackaye, p. 261.

175 still a Democrat, though very still": Fowler, p. 332.

176 "I don't know. I haven't gotten the word yet": Kessner, p. 246; Walsh, pp. 332–333.

177 "O'Brien was not an idiot": Kessner, p. 246.

177 "the most effective leader in the House": *NYT*, November 15, 1932.

178 Lanzetta's victory: Brodsky, pp. 245–246.

178 Roosevelt's overwhelming victory: Kessner, p. 195.

178 "Exit One Gadfly": *NYT*, November 15, 1932.

179 "the importation of floaters and repeaters": Brodsky, p. 246.

179 "too old to take orders from anyone": Kessner, p. 197.

179 McKee's departure from politics: Mackaye, pp. 262–263.

180 Seabury seeks a candidate: Kessner, p. 241.

180 "You sold out to Tammany Hall!": Brodsky, p. 269.

Notes

181　"There is only one issue": Brodsky, p. 272.
182　"we cannot look for ideal results from such material": Brodsky, p. 278.
183　La Guardia's vote: Mann, pp. 142–143.
183　"there was not . . . a single person": Moscow, p. 126.
185　"the most tantalizing disappearance of our time": Manning.
185　"the outstanding disappearance of modern times": Churchill, p. 56.
186　*NYT* review of Stella's book: *NYT*, April 19, 1961.
188　"he had nothing to add to the files": *NYT*, September 15, 1971.
188　a "technicality": *New York*, August 11, 1980.

INDEX

Index

Index

Index

A NOTE ON THE AUTHOR

Richard J. Tofel is the assistant publisher of *The Wall Street Journal* and a vice president of Dow Jones & Company, publishers of the *Journal*. Over fifteen years at Dow Jones he has worked as assistant general counsel, assistant managing editor of the *Journal*, director of international development, vice president for corporate communications, and assistant to the publisher of the *Journal*. A graduate of Harvard College, Harvard Law School, and the John F. Kennedy School of Government at Harvard, he has also written *A Legend in the Making*, an account of the New York Yankees in 1939 that was widely praised. He lives with his family in Riverdale, New York.